D1246983

IMMUNOLOGIC PSYCHOLOGY
AND PSYCHIATRY

IMMUNOLOGIC
PSYCHOLOGY
AND
PSYCHIATRY

Wallace Marshall, M.D.

THE UNIVERSITY OF ALABAMA PRESS
University, Alabama

Library of Congress Cataloging in Publication Data

Marshall, Wallace, 1904-
    Immunologic psychology and psychiatry.

    Includes index.
    1. Neuropsychology. 2. Neuropsychiatry. 3. Learn-
ing, Psychology of. 4. Immunology. I. Title.
[DNLM: 1. Behavior. 2. Learning. 3. Neurophysiology.
WL102 M369i]
QP360.M35   612.8   75-8713
ISBN 0-8173-2703-7

Copyright © 1977 by

WALLACE MARSHALL, M.D.

Manufactured in the United States of America

Contents

Dedicated to
Louise and Victoria Louise

Acknowledgments

Whenever an author sets himself aside in order to concentrate on the completion of a book, his family members may find it difficult to accept his moody behavior. Louise, my wife, and Vicky, my daughter, have been most understanding throughout the lengthy episode that this book's preparation has entailed, and I am most appreciative for their constant support, consideration, and love.

So many distinguished former professors prepared me for this work, I deem it only proper to recall some of those illustrious names: Professors Joseph Jastrow and Clark Hull in psychology; Kimball Young, the great sociologist; and the anthropologist, Professor Ralph Linton.

A two-year externship in neurology under Professor Sigmund Krumholz, M.D., at Cook County Hospital, Chicago, gave me a sound basis in that specialty. The very first of my professors who taught me how to prepare my first article and had it published was Professor Cleveland J. White, M.D., of Chicago, who joined me in dermatologic research which led to the discovery of the Marshall-White Syndrome. The late Professor Chester J. Farmer, Sc.D., gave me a strong understanding of biologic chemistry. He continued his interest in my researches until his death a few years ago. Professor C. Neymann always encouraged me greatly as did Professor Theodore A. Watters, both of whom offered me assistant professorships in their departments of psychiatry (Northwestern and Tulane, respectively).

Professor Judith Feldman, Ph.D., a psychologist par excellence, and Professor Charles Watkins, M.D. were particularly helpful during my psychiatric fellowship at Louisiana State University Medical School and Charity Hospital in New Orleans. Professor Sidney Easterling, M.C., helped me better to understand clinical psychiatry while I was at The Central State Hospital, located at Pineville, Louisiana.

I am indebted to the editors and publishers of *Medical Times* and *The Journal of the Louisiana State Medical Society* for allowing me to use material from my articles. William L. Smith, M.D., the Editor-in-Chief, Mr. L. P. Patterson, the Managing Editor, and Mary Nell Williford, the Assistant Managing Editor for *The Journal of the Medical Association of the State of Alabama* were particularly helpful in allowing me to reproduce my articles in any manner deemed advisable. They have been of inestimable help in getting my papers published quickly all the years during which I have contributed to their fine *Journal*. M. Kathryn Jones, the Reference Librarian of the Lister Hill Library of the Health Sciences of The University of Alabama in Birmingham, has helped greatly by forwarding requested data promptly to me.

Professor Ronald Bradley, Ph.D., the Head of Neurosciences at The University of Alabama School of Medicine, has so kindly written the Preface and has offered suggestions for this volume. He has never been too busy to discuss subjects with me whenever the need arose. Such a distinguished colleague is invaluable.

Professor Robert W. Schaeffer, Ph.D., the Head of the Department of Psychology, and Professor Delos B. McKown, Ph.D., the Head of the Philosophy Department, both at the main campus of Auburn University, gave me highly important suggestions, for which I am most grateful.

My close friend, Professor Arthur R. Garrett, Ph.D., of the Biology Department, and Professor W. F. Vitulli, Ph.D., of the Department of Psychology, both at the University of South Alabama in Mobile, offered highly pertinent data which is deeply appreciated.

Professor Wiley Boyles, Ph.D., Dean of Sciences, and Professor Patrick Slattery, Ph.D., Head of Psychology at Auburn University of Montgomery, with Dr. Judd

Katz, have encouraged me continually to write this volume. They were particularly helpful by affording me opportunities to teach some classes in psychology, and thereby gave me the delightful opportunity for student discussions on much of the material contained herein. I am additionally indebted to Professor Slattery for the gracious Foreword that he has written to a book whose existence owes so much to his encouragement.

Mrs. Margaret Rice, a truly remarkable person, helped type and helped proofread this volume. Her strong sense of humor and intelligence made my task much easier to accomplish. My wife, Louise, also typed the manuscript and contributed much to our efforts. Mrs. Gladys Jernigan, of Baptist Hospital, kindly typed the book's glossary.

If I have inadvertently missed thanking other colleagues who helped, I offer my sincere apologies and my many thanks.

Foreword

In a style of communication reminiscent of the great learning theorist, Edwin R. Guthrie, Professor Wallace Marshall has provided an extremely readable and comprehensive analysis of what he terms "immunological learning theory." *Immunologic Psychology and Psychiatry* is informative and interesting both to the professional in psychology or related fields, and to the student or layman who desires to further his practical understanding of human behavior.

Dr. Marshall, who describes himself as "nothing more than a country doctor," has drawn from over 35 years of practical experience and scholarly study to compile what amounts to a very timely statement on both effective and pathological human behavior acquisition and maintenance. For those of us who anticipate spending our lives specifically dealing with and studying the human organism's activity, the approach of immunological learning theory can become an addition, an adjunct, or perhaps an instructional alternative to both the classical and the more recently evolved behaviorally-based learning theories. Regardless of our biases, this approach is worth consideration, especially since we are interested in human behavior.

While the medical model, used by Dr. Marshall, has been in disrepute during the last decade or so among us behaviorists, we must admit that Marshall—who is, after all, a physician—has nevertheless used the model in a justifiable fashion to further the reader's understanding of the nuances treated in *Immunologic Psychology and Psychiatry*.

The book handles the topic of immunological learning theory in a systematic fashion. Beginning with an introduction to the historical development of the theory and statements of the basic immunological principles, Marshall prepares his reader for the complex concepts which follow. Neurological aspects of behavior are then treated. Next, the additional and important concepts of *frustration, motivation,* and *anxiety* are discussed. Dr. Marshall concludes his book with considerations of the role of theory in general and his theory in terms of its specific utility.

Throughout the text, the reader cannot help but be impressed with the depth of Professor Marshall's experience. Numerous personal incidents are cited which add immeasurably to the breadth of treatment. Notably missing from the book are the tables, graphs, and statistical tests so frequently presented in support of theoretical positions. While Marshall believes that much in the way of empirical evidence exists to support immunological learning theory, he is by his own admission a researcher who has not had the inclination or the time to conduct statistical tests specifically to check the theory. Such work remains to be done by his students.

Many of his ideas and statements have been refined during his classroom sessions. Professor Marshall has taught from this book in manuscript form for several years. One takes pride in the feeling that he may have influenced Dr. Marshall to organize past years of published work into a single volume so that it would be available for future students.

September, 1976 PATRICK SLATTERY

Preface

The immune system presents an attractive biological analogy for learning and memory. Antibodies demonstrate the facility to recognize selectively, to remember, and to forget. However, some caution should be exercised in applying the molecular models of immunology to the activities of cells in the brain, for as yet we understand little of the macromolecular synaptic events subserving learning or memory as they relate to behavior. That memory is a function of the synapse is inferred by several lines of reasoning.

First, after many years of research there is no really convincing body of evidence which identifies the chemical nature of the "memory molecule." Protein, DNA, and RNA are certainly contenders for the title but even if the nature of the molecule is understood, how would such chemical coding be translated into a functional modification of brain function subserving behavior? Also, a considerable time is required to synthesize these molecules so they could hardly be involved in short-term memory. Perhaps the most interesting experiments on the nature of memory have involved the demonstration that when an animal acquires a simple task, a molecule may then be extracted from its brain and injected into a naive animal conferring upon it the ability to learn that task more rapidly. It is speculated that this molecule is a peptide and that it in effect contains the memory code for the task. However, although many experimenters have replicated this finding in several species and for many tasks, there are a smaller number of experimenters who are unable to find any evidence for such "memory transfer." The current status of this research may be summarized by saying that, if a "memory transfer" factor is unequivocally shown to exist, then it will have to be demonstrated that the

molecule is in fact a coded representation of a specific behavior. Alternatively it could be a hormone that merely
promotes learning in a general fashion or alters some other
physiological variable such as arousal or activity which
would in turn increase the probability of learning.

A second reason to consider membrane biophysics in the
mediation of learning is that rapid information transfer in
the nervous system is currently identified only with
membrane function in the form of polarization changes
mediated by electrochemical events at the synapse and
transmitted by voltage-dependent gating mechanisms as in
the action potential.

Third, the synapse is known to expand after learning and
there is a body of evidence to suggest that increased synaptic use gives rise to altered synaptic function.

Antibodies are of great significance for biochemistry
because they have the ability to recognize other molecules
often with greater sensitivity than any laboratory method
available to the scientist. This property has given rise to a
new chemical technique of enormous power named "radio-
immunoassay" which is currently making a unique contribution to the chemical study of the brain.

The concepts of immunology are already applicable in the
discussion of diseases of the nervous system. For example,
when the myelin sheath of the neurons is chemically
extracted from the nervous system and then injected into
normal animals, they soon become paralysed and die. This
happens because the immune system produces antibodies to
attack the invading myelin; but these antibodies cannot dis-
criminate, for they enter the animal's brain and destroy its
own myelin. This experimental allergic encephalomyelitic
(EAE), as it is called, may provide an animal model for
multiple sclerosis, a human demyelinating disease. At least
it offers the scientist a laboratory animal system which he
may use to study a progressively disabling brain disease
about which we know very little.

The same concept may be applied to the peripheral nervous system which communicates with our muscles. Those nerves, which cause muscles to contract, induce their influence by releasing Acetylcholine (ACh) from the nerve endings. This ACh is recognized by protein molecules called receptors located at the muscle endplate, and the reaction between ACh and its receptors results in muscle activity. When these proteins are extracted and then injected into normal animals, they induce the production of antibodies; but again the discriminatory process is inadequate. The antibodies deal with the invaders but also go to the muscles of the animal, where they attack his own receptors and cause paralysis. Such an experimental allergic paralysis may represent an animal model of the human neuromuscular disease myesthenia gravis. This area of neuroscience is only just beginning and holds much promise for our future understanding of brain function.

These animal studies suggest that some neurological diseases are caused by an abnormal immune system where the body turns upon itself and destroys its own nervous tissue by mistakenly treating its component proteins as foreign invaders.

In the study of memory, if and when a responsible molecule is revealed, antibodies for this molecule may be shown to induce behavioral change. These effects would of course be useful in clarifying the real function of such a molecule in the memory process. It has already been demonstrated that antibodies may be produced which selectively attack only one brain region, the caudate nucleus. In fact antisera to unique antigens found only in the nervous system are reported to produce behavioral effects in animals. It is even suggested that antisera to brain extracts from animals trained on certain tasks will interfere with the performance of similar tasks in recipient animals.

In dealing with psychopathology, Dr. Marshall offers a similar medical-biological analogy between the phenomena of allergic reactions and human behavior. He uses the language of allergy and immunology to comment upon many aspects of abnormal behavior including those psychological analogues of hypersensitivity which are especially relevant to the biological model in psychiatry.

Admittedly, given our present understanding in neurobiology, the locus of a "psychoallergen" in the brain is no more certain than the seat of the ego. But the near future must surely hold promise of detailed investigation in neuroimmunology which may verify the validity of the ultimate molecular analogy between immunoglobins and the "memory molecule." In the meantime this theory propounded by Dr. Wallace Marshall over the years will continue to be intriguing not only because it may be fashioned in the molecules of life but because it enables man to see his own behavior and that of his fellow man in the light of an inevitable and ultimately comprehensible biological system.

September, 1976   RONALD J. BRADLEY

IMMUNOLOGIC PSYCHOLOGY
AND PSYCHIATRY

Introduction

While it is hoped that this book will prove to be most salubrious to our readers, undoubtedly it will produce saltations which may prove quite disturbing to advocates of other current psychologic theories. Few colleagues will desire to forsake those teachings they have cherished over their professional years.

However, I believe many colleagues will now agree that the neural sciences will continue to contribute a great deal to psychologic and psychiatric knowledge. Many fresh and important facts have already come from such studies. Perhaps the patterns for future work in our field will demand comprehensive studies from the basic sciences that will call for increments in biology, physiology, anatomy, pathology, and immunology as these are applied to the various neural apparati and their functionings to understand behavior.

Many psychologists agree that the topics which deal with learning are of paramount importance. Neural scientists also concur that these topics are of prime interest in their scientific investigations. If we can really understand what the process of learning is all about, then we will have accomplished much to further our understanding of behavior. Learning theories might well comprise the first college course that should be offered in all departments of psychology. For the name of the game could be the firm understanding of learning, its processes and ramifications.

So far as I know, few textbooks in psychology and psychiatry have offered a sound relationship between normal and abnormal learning and its resultants as exemplified by normal and abnormal behavior. Our theory will attempt to explain these various behaviors in biologic terms that are well understood by the scientists. Past and current behavioral theories have employed nonbiologic nomenclature, whose meaning tends to vary among individual students of psychology. The same difficulty is found unfortunately in the field of psychiatry, where many psychiatrists harbor their own individual understanding and interpretation of such nonbiologic terms. Perhaps many misunderstandings in psychology and psychiatry arise from the Tower of Babel usage of a nonscientific terminology that exhibits philosophic overtones and concurrent misinterpretations, so that reliable communications break down between students of behavior. We hope this book presents a practical and workable theory of learning, and we trust that it explains normal and abnormal behavior together with results from clinical psychologic testing (diagnosis) and therapy.

As our treatise appears to be the first extended work on the psychoimmunologic approach to learning, mistakes are bound to occur. It is hoped that the readers will bring whatever inconsistencies they discover to our attention so that these can be clarified in possible future editions.

Much of the data presented has originated from the author's published papers and from lectures to his students in various psychology courses. Critiques from colleagues in philosophy, psychology, and the neural sciences have been duly considered and were incorporated. It is to be expected that others will not find it appropriate to accept some of the principles promulgated herein. However, I trust this volume will at least give them a new and possibly promising approach to their own concepts about the processes of learning and behavior. It is hoped that colleagues who are concerned with experimental approaches will duly test the psychoimmunologic theory. This cannot help but further our acceptance and understanding of those principles which this treatise presents. If additional research findings cannot fit readily and comfortably into the general matrix of our theory, then the psychoimmunologic approach should not be considered worthy of further attention. Contrarily and to date, the theory has been of inestimable value to many students and clinicians alike in assisting a ready understanding of those many mechanisms which are involved in learning and the formation of both normal and abnormal behaviors.

Some of my students have elected to take my courses in psychology because of their desire to understand why a particular behavior ensues. The following should not be construed as an *argumentum ad hominem,* particularly against the teachings of B. F. Skinner, who appears interested mainly in what goes into and out of The Skinner Box. Rather, we must also concern ourselves not alone with mere stimuli and the responses they invoke but with what actually happens within the box; in other words, we should formulate some practical concept about the central mechanisms (cerebration) which control responses. One can hop on a bicycle, pedal it, and it moves. But if we remain unconcerned about the mechanics involved with bicycle riding, we might become very upset should the driving chain disintegrate. If we do not know how a bicycle works, its repair becomes an impossibility. The same argument holds true with other functioning parts, such as with a malfunctioning automobile, a plant which begins to wilt, or an erstwhile placid-tempered individual who suddenly becomes highly hostile. Otherwise, individuals—and students in particular—can become *aux abois.* We may not be able to give proper answers to all the many complexities which involve normal and abnormal behavior, but at least we shall make a brave attempt to do so with whatever new knowledge becomes available.

One of the main uses for the theory should be to serve as a construct, loose enough to allow the student or practitioner to add to it without difficulty as modern data becomes available. During the nearly forty years the author has been formulating this theory, he has not had to change the basic principles. The only main revision has been the change from the term *psychoallergy* to the term *psychoimmunology* in order better to clarify the approach used by the theory. The latter term is not so confining, since it denotes the body's reaction to injury which can be produced by bacterial infection as well as those bodily reactions observed with the physical allergies. Hence, *psychoimmunology* is more inclusive for describing those processes related to the reparative processes of the body that result from injuries of all sorts, including those that affect the psyche and soma.

The reader should find the *modus operandi* of the immunologic approach to behavior relatively easy to understand and apply in everyday life, after the theory's nomenclature and principles have been mastered, just as discovering the key to a difficult code can unlock its seeming impossibilities. Hindsight is much easier than foresight. When one contemplates the years which passed before a practical behavioral insight occurred in our field, it will become apparent that the study of immunologic principles has contributed much in overcoming this impasse.

If a reasonable learning theory explains behavior readily without the use of the 42 Hullian postulates, this might be viewed as progress. However it means that the teacher must acquaint himself with immunologic principles and with the many teachings which are to be found in the neural sciences—a course that has not been followed in most departments of psychology. Present and future students in this field must be prepared properly by taking more courses in physics, biology, chemistry, anatomy, physiology, and immunology if they are to survive the rapid changes occurring in the behavioral fields.

Psychology is a science in its own right, and it is necessary to understand molecular neural changes that result from learning if the student is to be prepared properly and adequately for his future role in this scientific discipline, whether in investigative or clinical psychology. Students should be able to confer readily with their fellows in other fields without the marked disadvantage of not having mastered the terminologies employed by other scientific modalities—an already manifest deterrent to scientific progress in behavioral studies.

How well I recall taking my canines to the older veterinarians during my childhood. Those doctors employed terms that were completely foreign to the human fields of medicine. However, all this changed. As one professor in a school of veterinary medicine told me, "We are the last to apply what has been learned in medicine. The original work often came from research on dogs, but we seem to be on the tail end when it comes to the dissemination of such scientific information." The final result has been the conversion of the older veterinary nomenclature to that employed by physicians, so that, currently, many canine disorders have counterparts involving terminologies applied also to human disorders, such as the allergies, the various heart diseases, brain tumors, fractures, etc.

The entire fields of science should have terminologies which are understood readily by all scientists. Psychology and psychiatry should offer no exceptions.

The introduction of the study of immunology to the field of psychology should provide another important tool for further research in many psychologic investigative endeavors. Such an addition to the current armamentaria cannot but broaden many psychologic approaches and viewpoints. All these should bring psychologists, and the nomenclature they employ, closer to other scientific fields, to assist mutual comprehension. This in itself should bolster the status of psychologists among other scientists.

Students in psychology must broaden their studies if these future investigators are to become equipped adequately to make new approaches to the studies of learning and behavior. Similar changes must also take place with students of psychiatry. The neural sciences must play dominant roles in preparing students for accomplishments in both psychology and psychiatry.

Although it is impossible to present detailed expositions, within this volume's confines, of such fields as neural physiology, neural anatomy, neural pathology, and immunology, it is hoped that a synoptic review of at least the salient features of these fields will be understood by the reader, as it is essential that the reader comprehend their application to our theory. If further information is desired, the reader is advised to consult the various plentiful sources, such as textbooks and articles, which abound in most university libraries.

One word of caution should be mentioned. Much of the teachings in this book are original, and are taken chiefly from articles I have written. Each chapter offers a list of references that will lead the reader to source articles in the professional journals.

Our volume's main thrust can be summarized by stating that it will offer a practical theory for behavior which has been and can be employed clinically. Biologic nomenclature is used; more or less nebulous or philosophic terminology is avoided. This practice conduces to an acceptable exchange of data between the various scientific fields. Currently, such exchange is often difficult, sometimes impossible.

It has been my unfortunate experience, when discussing various topics with some psychologic and psychiatric colleagues, to have been subjected to loquacious explanations. However, when the air cleared from the barrage of verbiage and jargon, very little information resulted. Each brand of psychologic and psychiatric theory has its particular neology. Their protagonists usually demonstrate adequately a colloquial connotation commonly known as "the gift of gab," but their explanations for certain behavioral aspects leave one with a definite feeling of emptiness. We ask finally, "What did they really say?"

In this volume, I hold to terminology accepted in most of

the scientific fields. The terms employed should be comprehended without difficulty as to their actual interpretations and meanings, which are set forth in this volume's glossary.

In Memory of Mike

Using immunologic principles, we begin our study of behavior with a true story. I trust it will focus the reader's attention on a problem of paramount importance, and of very recent vintage.

Mike was a wiry, very sensitive lad of sixteen who had lost his dad at an early age. So Mike was raised amidst a number of kindly females and his doting mother. But he missed having a father around the house. He spoke about this situation many times. When an opportunity arose to join the Marines, he finally convinced his mother to let him go, because he wanted to be with other men, to grow up.

After his basic training, he was sent to Vietnam. But he was not prepared for the bloody, painful, and cruel scenes he observed. These highly carnal episodes affected him deeply. He became hypersensitized to bloodbaths.

Finally he received an honorable discharge from service, and he married his childhood sweetheart. He obtained a job, but was not enamored of his work; so he finally succeeded in obtaining a new one where he could use his managerial capabilities.

However, his wife had noted that Mike showed mood changes; he would become depressed, and during these times he would tell his wife of his burning desire to kill—anyone, as a matter of fact. One time he placed two shells in a revolver and pulled the trigger as he aimed at his very young son and his wife. Luckily, the gun didn't discharge. Other times, when his son was in bed, Mike would make the lad deliver Karate chops to his wife and himself. Her protestations were not heeded by Mike, who seemed to have a pressing desire to teach his son how to defend himself. This was understandable, since Mike had been horribly injured by those nightmarish Vietnam events, and he wanted his son to be able to defend himself, which Mike felt he himself was incapable of doing.

Mike often spoke about his buddies who had died in that war, and he repeatedly asked why he was spared from death.

One day Mike received a gentle rebuff from his employer, who urged Mike to do better with his sales. This came soon after the boss had told him of his great pleasure when Mike had landed a large sale. Unfortunately, this business venture fell through, and Mike again became depressed, deeply.

Soon after this, while his wife and child were visiting out of town, Mike swallowed every sort of pill he could find. He locked all the doors of the house, went to his bathroom, and shot himself in the head. His body was discovered four days later. . . .

If we must cite a moral for this story it would be that we prepare our lads to fight for their country, but unfortunately we do not screen them sufficiently. Sensitive lads like Mike cannot take bloody battle scenes which tend to push sanity into insanity. When they return home to their dear ones, they have not been freed from their urges to kill. Mike's story illustrates what can happen. The same chain of horrible events has destroyed other veterans. Why do such things happen to kindly and sensitive young men? Perhaps we shall discover the reasons as we progress through this volume. In any event, further extensive research is needed to diagnose and to treat adequately the depressed and unfortunate souls who have served their country well in time of war and peace. The Mikes, with countless others, must not continue to die in vain. Deep depressions often follow multiple frustratory events and, as we shall discover later, often end with complete and final frustration—death at one's own hands! Nothing is more baffling for psychologists and psychiatrists so far as adequate therapy is concerned.

Since this volume was written, E. A. Luria and J. V. Domashneva (*Proc. Nat. Acad. Sci.*, U.S.A. 71:235-36, Jan., 1974) announced the discovery of antibodies in the sera of schizophrenic patients. These antibodies act against thymic antigens localized on thymocytes and thymus-derived lymphocytes. These findings strongly support our immunologic theory of behavior.

1

History of
Immunologic Theory

Back in the '20s when I studied psychology under Professors Joseph Jastrow and Clark Hull, behaviorism was in full swing. Although I became enamored with behaviorism, it did not explain basic events, such as learning and personality. My questioning of its teachings led me to study the basic sciences, such as physiology, neurology, and physiological chemistry.

One particular problem troubled me, and that was psychology's inability to relate normal to abnormal behavior, since no particular theory in psychology seemed adequately to answer this pressing question. This became all the more troublesome to me when I studied psychopathology and then psychiatry in medical school.

One day, while in a seminar in sociology under famed Professor Kimball Young, the concept of the sensitivity of each human individual hit me. Why hadn't any investigation even mentioned this point? Although Dr. Young was interested in this question, he offered no definitive answer. So the quest began to find some suitable answer somewhere.

After my internship, and following several years in general practice and surgery, I was given the opportunity to teach physiological chemistry and introductory medicine at the Medical School of The University of Alabama. That year (1936-37) afforded me plenty of occasion to return to those questions which haunted me in psychology.

At that time, I termed my approach the psychoallergic

theory. In a paper published in the *Medical Record,* I attempted to explain and correlate the *modus operandi* of routine biologic phenomena with those of psychology and psychopathology. I tried to reduce behavioristic, Gestalt, and Freudian teachings to biologic reactions.

There were points in Dashiell's conditioning theory of behavior which bothered me thirty-six years ago and still do to this day. In this *Medical Record* paper, I wrote of points in the Stimulus-Response Theory which need further explanation. A few examples are:

1. What keeps the neural pathways from getting mixed and "shorting"?
2. What determines which pathway a stimulus will travel in this intricate maze of neural associations and interlocking tracts?
3. Why does an apparently insignificant sensory stimulus at times cause a great response in an individual?
4. Why are there so many individual differences to similar situations?

I believe the immunologic approach will answer most of these questions as my reader progresses in his understanding of just how this theory operates. My students usually experienced difficulty understanding our approach until they mastered the terminology. From then on, the theory seemed very simple to comprehend; and it is applicable to the clinical aspects of abnormal behavior which I observe daily in my psychiatric practice.

Studies in allergy and immunology emphasize the body's reaction to injury. Even a small stimulus can evoke a much larger response when the subject has become hypersensitized. This does not occur in normal individuals.

So it appeared to me that the learning process was related to these immunologic findings, since learning did not consist only of the basic stimulus→response reaction of the behaviorists. A stimulus could be tiny or large in caliber (dosage) and the resulting response could be small or overwhelming, which depended upon the nature of the sensitivity or hypersensitivity encountered in each individual.

Besides these points, what effects were produced by previous related stimuli? Had these subsequent doses of similar stimuli caused an increase in the reactions of such an individual?

Was this a new form of response produced by one's hypersensitive state? This appeared to occur also with the learning processes, for once a particular stimulus from one's environment became registered in the brain, that individual reacted differently to similar stimuli. In other words, learning had taken place because of the effects of sensory stimuli upon the brain which had supplied it with information from the individual's environment. This takes place in normal subjects but it does not occur in certain amentias, where disease has destroyed a part or all of the sensitive neural tissues.

My first attempt to present the psychoallergic (psychoimmunologic) concept appeared in a paper published in the *American Journal of Psychiatry* (2). In this article was my concept of learning, which was composed of various allergic (immunologic) reactions to toxic stimuli (1). This point seemed to closely link normal and abnormal psychology with biology through the important consideration of sensitivity.

A few years later, in 1938 I presented a paper before The American Psychological Association at Ohio State University. The paper's title was "The Immunologic Concept of Learning" (3) and the resume follows:

"This paper presents the physiological implications of the learning processes from a new point of view. With the brain cells possessing a marked degree of sensitivity (as can be measured with the E.E.G.), the point is made that afferent stimuli, whether they are visual, acoustic, olfactory, etc., seem to sensitize the particular areas of the brain which have to do with the perception of the particular nerve tracts in question. Added stimuli cause further sensitizations of these areas, and learning takes place through the immunological mechanisms of cellular response to irritation. The point is brought out that the synapses are a secondary consideration; for the caliber of the stimulus (size), plus the number of stimulations, plus the nature of the recording centers in the brain (normal or pathological), determines such factors as the rapidity and apptitude of the learning processes. From the normal phase of learning, it is understood readily how pathological syndromes arise, such as residual hypersensitized reactions to certain key words, as exemplified by what Freud terms 'complexes'. This new concept of learning ties the normal with the abnormal manifestations, and explains the physiological nature of the amentias, word blindness, etc. It opens new avenues of attack on this subject and suggests new clinical and laboratory procedures in order to gather further data on such problems.

Additional papers on the theory were published (3, 4, 5, 6, 7, 8) with perhaps a few more similar ones which have become misplaced or lost throughout these many years.

It was around 1950, while serving *Medical Times* as its Research Editor, that I accidentally discovered what Priestley and his great teacher, Hartley, had taught about the time our nation was being founded.

At that period in my professional career I searched in many out-of-the-way places for all the old medical volumes I could find. I happened to cross upon Joseph Priestley's volume (9), which I avidly purchased, since I recalled that he discovered oxygen. Priestley followed Hartley's theory that the brain received stimuli from the sensoria in the form of "vibruncules" or tiny neural waves. This concept was all the more remarkable since at that time little was known about how stimuli affect afferent nerves (which connect one's environment with the brain) nor about the transmission of neural impulses.

Basically, the Hartley-Priestley concepts were definite

forerunners of the psychoimmunologic theory. These early scientists argued that the nerve and brain substances were quite similar, and sensations, as perceived by the brain, were transmitted by the incoming nerves. They called their theory the Association of Ideas. It is regrettable that these teachings had become lost with time, for their principles might have enriched the subsequent Pavlovian Theory by focusing on what took place in the cerebral cortex as the result of sensory stimuli impinging upon the cortical cells because of their common property of neural sensitivity.

In 1966, I closed my office for the general practice of medicine in order to concentrate upon psychology and psychiatry. An opportunity arrived whereby I became a fellow-resident in psychiatry in a well-known school of medicine and hospital to review what had taken place since my graduation from medical school. During this postgraduate work, it became overly obvious that great stress was being placed on Freudian and Neo-Freudian theories, which I was unable to accept and have not done so at any time during my practice of psychiatry and my teaching in psychology.

2

Immunologic

and Allergic

Principles

Immunologic and allergic principles will be employed to formulate our immunologic construct for explaining our approach to behavior. My readers should now be introduced to some basic concepts concerning the body's altered response or behavior which is acquired through contact with some factor that produces such an abnormal response. The re-exposure to this identical material produces irritability of the body in its reaction to this or related materials. This is termed an allergic reaction.

Many agents, such as certain foods, bacteria, pollens, drugs, and other toxic substances, are capable of producing abnormal reactions, such as hives, serum sickness, asthma, hay fever, and allergic rhinitis. Any of the above agents can act as antigens or allergens which, when introduced into an erstwhile normal human or animal, are capable of producing antibodies, causing an allergic episode by the interaction of antigen and antibody.

Antigens of protein nature can produce allergic responses. Furthermore, metals and drugs have been shown recently to be capable of reacting with body proteins, thereby forming new proteins which may be toxic in nature. These are also capable of setting off allergic reactions.

Allergens can enter the body through inhalation, ingestion, contact, and infection. Various physical allergens from heat, cold, and light may be capable of producing allergic reactions in some patients.

The phenomena involving allergic reactions are based upon the antigen (allergen)-antibody reactions, since the antigen causes the body to produce the specific antibody which combines with the allergen, antigen, or immunogen.

Allergists test allergic patients to determine what particular agents are involved to produce the patient's hypersensitized state. This is accomplished often by means of scratch tests where various skin areas are scarified (scratched) and certain antigens are rubbed into these areas. The offending antigens or allergens can produce reddened and swollen skin areas, whereas materials, which are not acting as allergens or antigens, do not produce such reactions in the scarified skin areas, which may be examined within minutes or days. Usually the positive skin areas, which are red and swollen, may also produce itching (pruritis) in a sensitive individual. Thus, allergy or an allergic state denotes an exaggerated response in a living organism by exposure to foreign substances which can produce a hypersensitive state in the affected individual.

Anaphylaxis (respiratory reaction) is produced by a primary injection of a foreign protein, which is followed by a repeated injection of the same protein material from 10 to 14 days later. This can produce a very severe reaction in the affected individual, and if not treated adequately might cause one's death. These responses of bodily mechanisms to foreign agents are important to understand because these responses will be employed to explain our approach to normal and abnormal behavior.

Immunity denotes the body's resistance or the body's defense against foreign materials or substances that are capable of producing antibodies in the affected individual which may rid the body of harmful antigens. So immunity also involves the antigen-antibody reaction.

Haptens can determine the immunologic specificity of the

antigenic molecule. Polysaccharides and arsenilic acid derivatives, which are not proteins, can react without or within the individual with antibody as can amino-acids, acetyl glucosamine, which are haptens. These are not the usual antigens one observes during daily practice but, if introduced in the body, they are capable of producing antibodies.

From what has been related, two important points stand out. Body reactions to antigens are specific and they take time to form antibodies. The initial introduction of an antigen begins the process of sensitization, and an additional dose is capable of producing hypersensitizations. The body reacts by *remembering* that it had become sensitized previously to that specific antigen.

Using a similar construct, neural impulses, originating within one or more sensory nerve tracts, bring environmental information to the central nervous system. These neural impulses can be considered to act similarly to antigens and are called psychoantigens, psychoallergens, or psychoimmunogens. They produce neuroelectrochemical changes in the cells of the brain and possibly the spinal cord. These neural stimulations cause the recipient brain centers to respond to such stimuli. A primary stimulation can sensitize the brain and subsequent specific stimuli may produce hypersensitizations in the recipient brain cells.

To date, no antibodies have been found in those bodily sensitizations which have been produced by any of the physical allergies, such as are produced by heat, cold, or pressure. Similarly, no antibodies have as yet been found which result when psychoantigens produce neuroelectrochemical brain cell changes which may result in learning. But future investigations may show the presence of antibodies produced both from reactions caused by the physical allergies and from reactions produced by psychoantigens (psychoimmunogens).

The desensitization procedures for both of the above

immunologic reactions are quite similar, and consist mainly of employing very minute doses of the offending agents, gradually increasing the dosages, until the individual does not react clinically to such antigens. Similar desensitizing therapy is employed also for other allergens which have produced hypersensitizations.

Immunology is the study of the biologic aspects which have to do with immunity, which an individual has or may obtain to render himself harmless to diseases, poisons, or infections or to other harmful influences or agents. An *immunogen* can produce a specific antibody against such a noxious agent or substance. This is a form of immunity. An *antigen* is a material which is able specifically to react with an *antibody,* or in certain circumstances can produce an antibody.

An *allergy* is a form of disease where a specific sensitivity becomes increased to an allergen or a hapten. Allergies are produced often by delayed states of sensitivity from contact allergens or the immediate forms of sensitivities because of Prauschnitz-Kustner antibodies. So it appears that the term *immunology* seems to be more encompassing than *allergy,* especially for our purposes.

For this reason, our concept of hypersensitivity, and how the neural structures react to it, should be changed from Psychoallergy to Psychoimmunology to be more explicit (1). Immunity is related to an individual's ability to overcome or resist infection. It was produced by some form of trauma, which involved the expenditure of energy. Immunity can protect the body from injury. An immune individual is free from such a threat to his welfare or wellbeing.

Relationships of Allergenic and Immunologic Factors to Behavior (2)

General Denominators. Some years ago, a comprehensive study was made on this subject (3). Perhaps only the passage of time changed the nomenclature in diagnosing psychotics, for the results of this study remain basically unchanged. The role of heredity appeared to play a more dominant part with allergies than with the psychoses. In patients in the first decade, the allergies occurred more frequently than the psychoses. The factor of sex showed variance in allergic and psychotic patients: pubertal and menopausal changes were prominent in both forms of disorders, which also showed similar types of onset and of periodicity; and their degrees of severity appeared to influence their prognoses. Also, general health status influenced both forms of these disorders, for lowered resistance increased their liability to such diseases. Psychic factors and the multiplicity of sensitivities were inherent in the allergies and psychotics. Intercurrent diseases appeared to cause improvement in both types of these disorders, while sensitizing and provocative doses of antigens and/or psychoimmunogens might or might not enhance these disorders. Their sites of reactions in both diseases appear to be identical, and they appear to follow the same *modus operandi*.

Even eosinophilia can occur in the allergies and the psychoses. Finally, Jegorow's laws of allergy (4) seem to have exact counterparts in various psychopathologic disorders. *Specific Denominators.* Fish are the lowest form of life phylogenetically which are able to develop anophylaxis and, hence, Prauschnitz-Kitsner antibodies. Excessive amounts of these P-K antibodies can produce possible anaphylactic shock and death. Excessive emotional shock, such as intense fright, can whiten a person's hair prematurely as it can cause syncope or even death in certain cardiac patients. An example of what fright can do can be exemplified by placing a caged rabbit near a cage which contains a large snake. The rabbit will usually die of fright.

Employing some allergic and immunologic principles as described in several textbooks on these subjects (5), (6) various associations appear to exist between the subjects of immunology, learning, and psychotic states.

The matter of sensitivity is of particular importance in allergy, immunology, and psychoneurotic states. If sensitivity did not exist, no hypersensitivity would occur. Hence, certain allergens and antigens are quite capable of inducing states of hypersensitivity in certain individuals which result from bodily reactions to such noxious agents. These abnormal reactions are not found in non-sensitive individuals. One must always remember that the property of sensitivity is also the main characteristic of the entire nervous system, which responds to stimuli in normal subjects. This important ability keeps the organism in touch with its environment so it is capable of adjusting properly to changing and possibly threatening environmental situations. Without sensitivity to stimuli, the nervous system and also the immunologic mechanisms would become non-active and unreactive.

From the aspect of ontogeny, significant amounts of antibodies appear only after birth. Interestingly enough, this finding corresponds to the neonate's ability to learn properly. So far as antibody production is concerned, IgG antibodies appear from four to six weeks following human birth. This happens to be approximately the time when human infants begin to perceive stimuli from their environments, and the learning processes begin to function. Nelson (7) states that the infant can fix his gaze on a light or some other bright subject and follow this object with his eyes for a few degrees from the line of his vision within a month's age. He can follow it through a 180-degree arc by the end of the second month when the hand and eye coordination develop also. The infant may reach for and hold an object briefly by the end of twelve weeks. Perhaps the most important infantile progress is registered within eight weeks when the infant smiles as the result of his social contacts. These infantile reactions result from the baby's learning, mainly through what he sees, hears, tastes, smells, and feels.

The Montessori teaching method appears to have much merit, since it attempts to reinforce environmental stimuli through the sense of feel which accompanies visual and auditory stimuli, the two main avenues for learning. This same use for the sense of feel was employed in the famous case of Helen Keller. Tactile stimuli and their value to infant learning appear to have been overlooked until comparatively recently. Most parents will recall their infantile offspring putting every nearby object in their mouth. They were learning the nature of those objects from tactile stimuli. Similar behavior is observed with puppies, which seem to delight in tasting and chewing on every conceivable and nearby object to become acquainted with its characteristics and thus sensitize the recipient cortical centers through this imprinting process known as learning.

Recently a TV commercial depicted Buddy Hackett as a space man, emerging from his space craft. He seized a package of potato chips and eagerly attempted to stuff them into his eyes, nose, ears, and finally his mouth. He then expressed marked satisfaction as he munched them and uttered sounds of pleasure. Perhaps this is a crude way of depicting the learning process, and I wonder if the Madison Avenue hucksters realized the scientific nature of their commercial.

Some tots appear to favor learning mainly through vision, while others seem to learn more proficiently through hearing and/or the tactile (touch) sensations. Early recognition of these preferred pathways for learning is highly important. Each child should be tested to determine the exact nature of his sensoria and the child's neural pathway preference concerning the ability to learn. The early recognition of possible sensory defects will pay off handsomely in later life, particularly when the children reach school age. Obviously, hereditary factors favor certain neural and brain proficiences as well as the various neural and brain deficiencies as with dyslexia (alexia). With present learning methods, all children are taught with one rigid procedure, which, in itself, is not too physiologically sound.

Prompt early diagnostic procedures for possibly deficient afferent and cortical neural pathways may do a great deal to locate and correct such deficiencies at the earliest opportunity. If such corrective measures become delayed, or if possibly questionable therapeutic procedures are employed by improperly trained personnel, further damage may result in these affected children. Some remedial procedures have not received expertise ratings by qualified scientists and medical clinicians. Moreover, some of these questionable therapies have proved to be exhorbitantly expensive so that only very wealthy parents can properly finance such work and gain advantage therefrom as a type of status symbol. One cannot turn back the clock with the ontogeny of any individual so that current training will compensate for that allegedly missed during his neurologic development. However, reeducative therapies which substitute a properly functioning afferent neural tract for a deficient one does make much sense. Such was employed with marked success in Helen Keller's case, for cases with Parkinsonian syndromes (8), (9), multiple sclerosis (10), Morvan's disease (11), and other neurologic disorders.

It is known that premature infants form fewer antibodies than do normal infants. A parallelism might also exist with the lack of proper neural maturation so they might learn as do normal infants; whether the placental barrier has anything to do with these ontological processes is not known presently.

The opossum develops antibodies around the 20th day of gestation. It would be interesting to learn if this process is related in any manner to the recognition of fetal stimuli (in utero). A relationship is known to exist between antibody formation and the development of lymphoid tissue. All this may later be shown also to correspond to the recognition of fetal stimuli, which can be regarded as a very early stage of the learning processes in such animals. A definite correlation exists in the decline of antibody formation in the human with a similar decline in learning ability around the age of 60.

Immunologically immature animals are presumed to acquire immunologic tolerance to intrinsic "antigens of self" which are capable of producing autoimmune diseases such as Hashimoto's thyroiditis, lupus erythematosis, immune hemolytic anemia, and experimental allergic encephalomelitis. Some observers think that certain types of idiocy may be related to the formation of autoimmune bodies *in utero* or during an early age neonatally, and from the inheritance of abnormal genes.

Heath's Views on Schizophrenia

One of the most encouraging series of recent studies on this baffling psychosis has come from Heath's laboratories at Tulane. He views this disorder as caused by structural changes produced by ataraxin. This pathologic substance appears to be generated by faulty predetermined genetic factors (12). Heath stresses the concept that a person's behavior is produced from his previous experiences, such as memory resulting from sensory perception. This is exactly what the psychoimmunologic theory stresses. The individual, states Heath, is programmed by early environmental stimuli which produce his experiences. Heath believes that ataraxin, obtained from schizophrenic patients, may be "antibody to unique antigenic sites of the septal region" in such patients. Incidentally, Heath is one of the very few psychiatrists who has mentioned the importance of learning, per se, in the genesis of mental disease.

Concerning brain antigens, Mihailovic and Hankovic (13) made immunologic techniques possible in studying brain macromolecules. Edelman and McClure used general fractionates of antigenic components in aqueous rat brain extracts. They found that the serum proteins were superior antigens (immunogens) to whole rat brain extracts. Electrophoresis of rat brain extracts against rabbit antiserum yielded eight to twelve brain antigens. But Bogoch discovered a minimum of thirteen brain antigens with the use of immunoelectrophoresis.

Concerning a possible explanation for the various psychologic processes, Schmitt proposes an interesting viewpoint (14). A gene (or RNA polymerase) is activated by ionic fluxes associated with excitation processes that act on the cell membrane area where sensory input impinges. This produces a permanent change in the membrane and forms a basis for feedback and recall. This model may serve as a chemical basis for psychologic phenomena, for these brain macromolecules may serve as the sources for fixed charges on membrane surfaces which may be responsible for electrokinetic phenomena. These macromolecules may be the sites of impedance changes which accompany physiologic transients including stored information (resulting from encoding).

Primary and Secondary (Memory) Responses to Antigens

A primary response to an antigen occurs possibly with the formation of antibodies to that antigen. When a second dose of the same antigen is administered months or even years later, an accelerated and intense bodily reaction occurs which is termed the ''specific secondary response'' or the ''memory response.'' These two forms of reactions occur with the administration of a specific antigen. Apparently the body recognizes the specificity of the particular antigen employed with each dosage of the particular antigen.

A similar response can be observed with the primary introduction of a sensory stimulus (psychoimmunogen). When an additional dose of the same type of stimulus is reintroduced, additional rapid learning may ensue. Perhaps the encoded cortical cells recognize the additional dose of related psychoimmunogen and reinforced learning takes place.

It is of interest to recall that antibody response diminishes with the age of the individual as does the ability to learn, especially in people past 60, as has been mentioned previously.

Anamnestic Response

This term was employed to denote the "recall production" of antibodies which are supposedly specific for one antigen through the administration of an unrelated antigen. Recent findings now suggest that these antibody responses are specific reactions to specific or closely related antigens which act on similar antigen determinant sites. Although not readily evident in nature, this anamnestic response is a protective one which undoubtedly occurs and whose importance cannot be overemphasized.

Also of major importance is the size of the primary antigenic or psychoimmunogenic dose. This reaction may well determine both the intensity and the period of longevity for memory. As an example, intense fright produced by a snarling canine may rapidly hypersensitize a child's cerebral cells and result in marked imprinting that may become lifelong as to fear of dogs.

From a therapeutic viewpoint, desensitization of such a hypersensitized state can take place through what Wolpe (15) has termed reciprocal inhibition, which is really a form of desensitization. To overcome the child's fear of dogs, small doses of psychoallergens (seeing the dog) are introduced to the phobic child. The dog is brought closer each time until the child's fears are allayed and he can pet the dog. This identical procedure was employed by the writer recently with a playmate of my daughter. This lad became hysterical every time our puppy happened to be nearby. He became desensitized to his fear with the passage of time until the dog and he became close friends.

A similar reaction and its therapy has been experienced by this writer and his surgeon father. During childhood, we both experienced nausea at the sight of blood. Later in life (during medical school) we both gradually became desensitized to this fear; however, this feeling of nausea returns at the sight of blood, and we have found it necessary to keep desensitized by periodically partaking in some operative procedures. I have been told that such reactions are not too rare among some surgeons who also have experienced hemophobia.

Antigenization and the Latent Period

This reaction occurs when antigens react by producing antibodies. Antigens may or may not incite specific antibodies. We can regard antigenization as taking place during the encoding process in the cortical cells as the result of psychoimmunogenic introduction.

A latent period of several days occurs usually between antigenization and the acquisition of tolerance with its antibody formation. This phenomenon has been also called immunologic tolerance, tolerance, antigenic paralysis, immunologic suppression, antigen tolerance, and immunologic unresponsiveness. It is supposedly caused by the failure of the antibody response to an antigen following the exposure to antigen. In other words, this tolerance is produced from prior exposure to antigens or closely related antigens.

A correlation appears to exist with the process of learning. For example, a bloodhound will not track if he has not been taught to use his marked sense of smell for recognizing human odors. But once the bloodhound is taught (perceives human scents) he shows marked ability to track. This is another example of perceptual reinforcement of learning. However, certain canines show a different reaction to learning, which might well be associated with inherited abilities.

The pointer remains rigid as he points at a bird. Such a latent reaction might be associated with a latent period such as accompanies antigenization. The latent period is also exemplified by the frozen positions taken by fighting cocks as they face each other, or by the periods of catatonic-like rigidity observed with cats during the times they are engaged in stalking their prey.

Psychologists have been baffled by this most intriguing phenomenon. Hebb (16) called this the "autonomous central process." But other terms include set, purpose, insight, attention, attitude, need, vector, preoccupation, perservation, expectancy, and hypothesis. Hebb considers this phenomenon as a recognition that responses are determined by something other than the immediately preceding sensory stimulation. Hull considered it as a stimulus trace set up by a lasting cerebral state, produced by some specific stimulus which is not transmitted or abolished immediately. This reaction certainly affects behavior, but it is not a part of an afferent stimulus according to Hull's conception.

Hebb's point is that neural excitation in itself does not explain set. In this writer's opinion, the psychologists are trying to explain the refractory state which is described herein. This lapse in overt behavior is readily explained in immunologic terms, as when previously sensitized cortical cells (previously encoded) now recognize an influx of associated neural stimuli (psychoallergens) and become refractory temporarily so far as observable behavior is concerned. In other words, the refractory period or set results from a sensitizing process in the affected cortical cells in both psychologic and immunologic states. Such a process is observed commonly whenever an individual is confronted with overwhelming doses of afferent stimuli (psychoallergens) which bombard some previously sensitized cerebral area and render the individual speechless (overwhelmed by the marked influx of associated psychoallergens). Also, such a refractory state in animals and birds, which are overcome by fright, might allow for their capture by predators.

Higher animals have the capacity to develop antibodies against a near infinite number of foreign bodies (antigens) whether harmful or not. It is assumed that a near infinite number of psychoallergens can either sensitize or hyper-sensitize the brain cells similarly, depending upon the size of the afferent dosage and whether the encoding cortical cells have been sensitized previously by allied psychoallergens.

Antigen Competition

It is known that when two or more antigens are introduced at or near the same time, the antibody response to one or more of these antigens may be repressed. This appears to also be the case when two or more afferent factors (psycho-immunogens) are introduced to an individual. Usually one will be dominant so far as learning is concerned. For example, a dose of psychoimmunogen via the visual tract may prove to be more dominant than a dose of psychoim-munogen via the auditory tract. Or this may be reversed in other individuals. Such preference may be related to one's innate abilities because of hereditary factors, the state of health in particular neural pathways and cortical areas, or other factors involved in the study of aptitudes.

However, antigen competition takes place usually when a strong antigen or psychoallergen is administered in a large dose hours or days before another similar antigenic dose is given. Strong antigens or psychoallergens appear to be more competitive than weaker ones. Hence, the dosage, the strengths, and the previous introduction of the competitive antigen or psychoallergen, with the time element, strongly affect the host's type of reaction to their introduction. Genetic factors also play highly important roles in the host's reactions as do various environmental aspects. All antigens do not elicit uniform immunologic responses. Marked differences in quantitative and qualitative response to antibody formation result from antigens among individuals of even the same species. The absence of a proper bodily response to a virulent antigen or psychoallergen may eliminate that individual from the population.

Importance of Physical Allergies

When Lewis (17) stroked the normal skin of patients with a hard object, he obtained the famed "triple response": the stroked skin areas responded to such stimulations by producing a reddened and slightly swollen area in their integuments. Stroking the skin with a blunt pencil produces what is known as dermatographia or skin writing, considered by many dermatologists a form of physical allergy.

Obviously, two topics should be considered relative to the above procedure. One has to do with the triple response of the skin to stimulation (touch and pressure). The skin receptors send neural impulses to the spinal cord which ascend the midbrain and cortex (afferent components) and downward through the spinal cord and to the muscles of the affected area (efferent system) where the body would naturally attempt to encope this scraping sensation, particularly if it proved to be excessively painful. Hence, the thalamic areas could well enter into such a situation caused by excessive skin stimuli that activated the pain-producing reactions.

It is believed that the triple response reaction of the skin is produced by the liberation of histamine, which causes the swelling and local reddening of the skin (hyperemia). A physical agent triggers the above responses, hence it is termed a physical allergy, which include bodily reactions to heat, cold, effort, and light. It is not known definitely whether definite antigens and antibodies occur in such a disorder. Sherman (18) has written a valuable volume on this subject as have Criep (19) and Rapaport and Linde (20); these supply data on the physical allergies. We are not at all sure that antigens and antibodies exist since these have not been isolated and identified chemically in the physical allergies.

The identical situation exists with environmental stimuli which travel the afferent neural systems to the brain and subcortical areas, and thence produce stimuli through the efferent tracts to the musculature where the affected organism tends to avoid further noxious afferent stimuli by either fighting or running away. Hence, we can note that quite similar situations and hallmarks occur in situations produced by the physical allergies and what we term the learning responses.

The fact that histamine occurs in the brain and can produce histamine headaches (21) is of interest when one considers the possible relationships which exist between the physical allergies and the hypersensitivites which may result from excessive afferent stimuli to the brain, as is the case with the Hullian concept of overlearning. Some experimental studies point to the effects on immunologic processes caused by stress factors. Anaphylaxis may influence those mechanisms which produce hypersensitivity in the central nervous system, and in some cases the hypothalamus can be involved. Suggestion apparently plays an important role in certain allergic diseases. Hypnosis also can alter allergic reactions, according to Engels and Wittkower (23).

Since histamine apparently plays a major role in the allergies, I performed a series of histamine desensitizations on schizophrenic patients. Several of my papers published in the late 1930's and 1940's disclosed positive results. Other investigators (Sakel and Sakel) followed my procedure with favorable results. However, the various shock therapies have succeeded histamine therapy.

3

Physiologic and

Neurologic

Principles

It is hoped my readers are abreast of previous work in physiological psychology, because I do not wish to spend much time on this topic, important as it is. Readers who lack a foundation in this phase of psychology are referred to Milner's excellent treatise on this important matter (1). For a more condensed review, the student is referred to Chapter 4 of Krech, Crutchfield, and Livson's excellent book (2).

The neuron is the basic unit of the nervous system structurally and functionally. Each neuron is composed of a cell body from which protrude filamentous, thread-like structures. These receive neural impulses from other nerve cells. Axones conduct nerve impulses away from the neuron.

The body of a neuron has a membrane around it to contain the shape of the neuron. This membrane exhibits the sensitivity that is a major characteristic of all normally functioning nerve to nerve impulses that appear to be electrical in character. The cell body of the neuron has a nucleus that is involved in the life-giving and life-sustaining processes of this nerve cell. The human contains several billions of such nerve cells that are in synaptic contact with certain of these neurones. Each neuron contains a fluid-like substance called cytoplasm which contains tiny folded membranes, termed Nissl bodies, containing ribonucleic acid or RNA. Mitochondria are smaller structures also found in the cytoplasm of the neuron, and the Nissl bodies and mito-chrondia are involved in the chemical matabolic changes occurring in the cell body.

Nerve Impulse Conduction

Although there are first, second, and third order neurones, located in certain portions of the neural tracts in nuclei, we are interested mainly in following the nerve impulses, originating from one's environment, to the recipient brain areas in normal individuals. Tumors, degenerated nerve tracts, and the like, can block these impulses from the brain—problems for the neuropathologist but not our present consideration.

Various electrical and chemical impulses produce responses in the cell membrane without injury to them. These impulses are very rapid and are conducted along the involved neural tract to receptor cells that contain a dendritic zone or surface and in some instances the dendrites themselves. These cells communicate with axons of other nerves, and so on, until a muscle or gland cell become stimulated to cause it to act. Before a neural cell acts, or is stimulated, it is in a resting phase, and the cell membrane keeps certain chemicals from entering the nerve cell. The tissue fluid outside the cell contains positively charged ions. But cell stimulation allows the positive ions to enter the nerve cell, producing a negative charge at the point stimulated, which, in turn, causes a nerve impulse that spreads rapidly along the nerve at its maximum intensity, according to the all or none law. A refractory period follows during which the nerve, having fired, is at rest.

Function of Synapse

Nerve cells come in contact with each other by means of synapses. My readers are urged to read Gardner's (4) excellent book on neurology. That volume presents important facts in a very concise manner.

Nerve impulses are transmitted from one nerve to the other at these synapses, where dendrites of one cell make contact with the axon of another neural cell by means of boutons that contain synaptic vesicles where further electric and chemical changes produce further transmission of a nerve impulse.

Most modern textbooks of psychology discuss synapses as the source for routing different stimuli. This process is invoked even to explain various types of behavior and also the process of learning; to this I cannot accede. The reasoning reminds me of a song, popular in the '40's, where "the music goes 'round and 'round and it comes out here!." Accordingly, the neural impulses also go round and round, and goodness knows where they will emerge. I believe synapses merely connect neural cells, allowing neural impulses from one or more afferent receptors to reach the recipient cortical cells where neuroelectrochemical changes ensue, thereby producing some form of learning.

It is important, however, to remember that, at excitatory synapses, the chemical transmitters are acetylcholine and norepinephrine, which depolarize the synaptic membrane. Hyperpolarization takes place for inhibition of the synaptic membrane. The nature of this transmitter still remains a mystery.

Some psychologists use a neural concept termed reverberation—whereby a neural impulse travels and retravels a neural circuit, especially within the brain—to explain memory of short term (5) that produces brain change. To my knowledge, few neurologic textbooks follow this line of reasoning. We shall discuss what we believe takes place as the processes of learning within the cortical and subcortical centers in a subsequent chapter.

4

Afferent

Nerve Tracts

At this point, we are concerned mainly with tracing neural impulses originating in the environment to the encoding brain centers. To this end, we shall first consider the many types of stimuli that can set up neural impulses. As psychology is a natural outgrowth of biology, we shall employ biologic terms to describe behavior, the better to relate psychology to biology, without use of the vague terminology that currently plagues both psychology and psychiatry.

Intrauterine Stimuli

Although human behavior provides our principal data, what follows is applicable also to other mammals and animals. All are endowed with inalienable inherited characteristics (1). Even in the womb the developing embryo or fetus receives warmth and pressure gradients (sustenance) from its mother. There is evidence of other prenatal stimuli which may affect the developing prenate, such as those which originate from noises, motion, and other stimuli, not to forget effects of placental origin, such as the incoming blood supply, which carries needed nutrients for growth and maintenance. Also, it has been shown that some noxious drugs can pass through the placental barrier. Heroin is one important example, since a mother addicted to it may well deliver a badly addicted offspring.

Throughout the entire course of neonatal development of

its anatomy and physiologic structures, forces (energy gradients) from the mother's environment play upon the mother, and her developing babe. These environmental stimuli may either benefit or harm the pregnant individual, depending upon the amount, the length of time these operate, and their possibly toxic nature. A pregnant mother who is the recipient of unwarranted beatings or who may be subjected to undue emotional stress can well be in very serious danger of aborting her fetus. Although nature has supplied the neonate with usually adequate defenses through its mother, who serves as a shield for her developing babe, an excess of harmful and painful stimuli can cause her to lose the developing neonate. Also, certain chromosome abnormalities of hereditary origin can produce irrevocable damage to the fetus.

The importance of prenatal sensory stimuli is currently recognized. Dubois (2) mentions that while still in their eggs, chicks are conditioned to some auditory and visual stimuli. After these chicks are hatched, they show varied responses to these same stimuli, whereas unconditioned chicks do not. Dubois writes about the influences which memory and heredity exert upon the individual. These influences produce permanent traces or imprints, called engrams. This is but another way of stating that learning affects the recipient cortical cells by producing the ability to use memory.

Neonatal influences from pressures (touch) and sound within the mother's uterus appear to play important roles in the behavior of the born individual (3). An example will help to clarify this point. From birth, my German Shepherd puppy, who was the runt of the litter, insisted upon sleeping on his back next to a wall, with his paws flexed upon his abdomen. This behavior baffled me until I recalled that some canine fetuses lie upside down and in the bottom position in the bitch's uterus. There the unborn pup receives pressure stimuli from the mother's uterine walls. After birth, the pup resumes his prenatal position, which presumably gives him a sense of well being. Identical behavior has been studied with human infants.

Trauma of Childbirth

Few pregnant women can deliver their offspring without experiencing some pain. Painless birth has been claimed by some obstetricians through the use of relaxation, drugs, suggestion and hypnosis. During my more than 30 years delivering mothers, I experienced only one case who delivered her child without any pain whatsoever and without the above pain-preventing measures.

The pregnant uterus, when at term and approaching the time for actual delivery, produces painful contractions from the dilating cervical os (opening) so that the oncoming fetal head can pass through it with uterine contractions which tend to push the infant through the uterine opening. These contractions tend to be more frequent, painful, and longer lasting. The head (skull) of the delivering infant contains fontanelles which tend to become molded to the mother's vaginal vault or outlet. Obviously, pressure from the mother's uterus must be painful to the emerging infant, particularly if the delivery proves lengthy.

The very first mother I delivered, on famed Professor Joseph B. De Lee's service at the Chicago Lying-In Clinic in the tenement district, took three days and nights. The child was delivered finally by Caesarian Section. This child must have experienced a great amount of trauma during such an extended interval of time.

When the delivering infant's head advances sufficiently along the birth canal, it might need to be turned from an upward to a downward position (from a posterior to an anterior presentation) to facilitate better delivery opportunities. This manipulation of the child whether by manual or instrumental means, is bound to produce additional pain. Forceps, when indicated, are applied to the oncoming head of the infant, and the child is carefully delivered. It is well to remember that the steel blades of the forceps, when clamped securely by the obstetrician, can put additional pressure on the child's head. At times, the forceps blades must be released to avoid excessive and prolonged pressure upon the fetal head.

When the child is delivered from its mother, the umbilical cord is securely clamped, then severed and tied, and a suction cup is inserted in the infant's mouth and throat to remove any foreign matter which could interfere with the infant's respiration. If the babe does not cry well, a pat on its rump may bring about the neonate's desired healthy cry.

I have seen new-born infants' mouths quiver and their tiny hands shake until they were placed in warm blankets. With all this trauma of birth, it is a wonder that there are so many normal infants and children! To add insult to injury, as the saying goes, the newborn child's eyes receive a diluted solution of silver nitrate (Crede). And later, if a male, the infant is usually subjected to circumcision, which has to be a painful procedure, although it is necessary to be accomplished properly for the child's welfare later in life. So it should go without saying that adequate prenatal delivery and postnatal care are highly important to protect both the mother and her child from unnecessary trauma and for the subsequent adequate development of the mentally and physically healthy pair, the mother and child alike!

The Ecosystem or Environment

When a child is born in a hospital delivery room, that room constitutes but a small part of the entire hospital. The hospital, in turn, makes up but a tiny part of the city where it is situated. We can continue this progression to the state in which one lives, then the entire country, then the entire world, and finally the universe.

However, these many items, taken collectively, make up the environment. Of more intimate importance is the immediate surroundings where one happens to find himself at some particular time. Place and people often surround the individual and, biologically speaking, form a major part of his immediate environment or ecosystem. But from a very broad viewpoint, the entire environment is important in the study of the structure and function of nature. This, the ecology certainly includes the living world (4).

Events of some sort occur almost constantly in an individual's immediate environment of places and people—his ecosystem. The individual can be affected directly because of the stimuli these events emit. A lighted, well-burning fireplace can produce needed warmth, a pleasurable occurrence. Or a burning splinter of wood that bursts from an ignited log can land on the livingroom rug and start a house fire which may well produce bodily burns and its consequent pain. One may enjoy a pleasurable sun bath on a beach, but too much sunshine can produce much pain. An overabundance of stimuli, coming from multiple sources, can cause the individual much pain. It is the size of the dosage from these stimuli, how long they are allowed to play upon the affected person, that determines whether pleasure or pain results. One milk shake, ingested by a hungry boy, may produce a sense of well-being. But the ingestion of multiple milk shakes within a brief time frame may cause him to experience marked gastric pain. Various aspects of an individual's nervous system are thus pleasured or pained by his ecosystem, whether he is at a lunch counter, or at church, or at home.

Sensitivity consists of the ability or the capacity of an organism to be stimulated or its capacity of being able to respond to stimuli acutely (5). Hence, the property of sensitivity appears to be an important attribute of stimulation. Similarly, a stimulus consists of any agent, act, or influence which produces a trophic or functional reaction in a receptor or within an irritable tissue or organ.

An ecosystem can be whatever part of the total environment that confronts man and his community of living and non-living matter. An ecosystem is but a small part of the environment where smaller ecosystems integrate and function within larger units.

These are controlled by homeostatic forces of nature which operate as checks and balances against undue oscillations within the environment. Also, there are individual and ecosystemic types of homeostasis which constantly tend to stabilize one's environment.

Some Ecosystemal Influences

The ecosystem with which an organism or individual comes in contact will greatly influence its behavior. Energy from such an ecosystem can stimulate and probably sensitize the individual's neural tube or brain, as the case may be, via its afferent connections. Thus, living in either a friendly or a hostile environment fashions the individual's behavior and way of life. A hostile environment predisposes the individual to either fight (aggression) or run (regression), types of behavior that depend heavily upon frustratory mechanisms which, in turn, are produced by painful situations. Defensive mechanisms are the *sine qua non* for survival in hostile ecosystems.

Ecosystemal energy may either stimulate or injure the individual. In other words, the dosage and the length of time environmental stimuli play upon the individual will determine the beneficial or the deleterious effects. For animals, sunlight, water, the atmosphere, and temperature are important for survival. Toward the end of his illustrious career, Sigmund Freud realized the importance of sunlight as the major sustainer for life, to the consternation of some of his psychoanalytic colleagues. However, the ecologists have long realized sunlight as being the ultimate source of energy for life's sustenance on this planet.

The Biological Clock

Ecologists speak of the photo period (length of the day), which directly influences the behavior of living organisms by what is known as the biological clock. This form of stimulus from the ecosystem acts upon the individual's hypothalmus by way of the optic tracts and produces a hormone which, in turn, stimulates the pituitary gland. This reaction releases, in sequence, several other hormones that act on various target organs. These series of reactions act similarly to a biologic clock, which is controlled by the length of the day— the period when light is available.

Ecologic Relationships to Psychology and Psychiatry

Obviously, an animal or human cannot perceive environmental change without an intact afferent nervous system which allows the individual to perceive these affects through his five afferent tracts or through substitutes for them. The seeing-eye dog is used by the blind human for the reason that his optic tracts do not function properly, as is the Braille system used by the blind in order to perceive printing through the use of the normally operating sense of touch. Nature has provided certain substitute compensatory measures whenever an afferent system becomes inoperable. As an example, the deaf person learns to lip read. Likewise the patient who loses a diseased kidney through surgery finds that the remaining organ enlarges to take over the functions of the removed kidney, via hypertrophy, as a compensatory measure towards the state of homeostasis.

The organism or the individual who, for any reason, fails to perceive the constant and varied changes which take place in one's ecosystem is in constant danger of being eliminated from the population, as can be observed, for example, from the country's high death rates on the highways. Here the ecosystemic road patterns change abruptly. A straight highway suddenly changes to a steep hill and sharp curve. Should the driver of a vehicle not perceive the warning signs, severe injury or death may ensue.

The excessive use of drugs and alsohol can dull the driver's perception involving sight, hearing, touch, and proprioceptive sensations so that he might drive on the wrong side of the road or leave the highway. Individuals unaware of railroad crossings can be mangled by oncoming locomotives. Car wreck victims' afferent systems had become dulled to the extent that they did not or could not perceive the numerous environmental changes which occurred constantly while their cars were moving at critical rates of speed.

One's inability to respond quickly and properly (involving prompt reflex responses) to environmental (ecosystemic) changes can lead to severe injury or death. One does not have to be driving a car to face such a dilemma. He can be putting gasoline in his car with a lighted cigarette in his mouth.

In other words, one's proper cerebration, coupled with adequate reflexes, are highly important for survival in coping properly with the many environmental (ecosystemic) changes which affect one's daily routine during the entire life span. This has and can end abruptly for those individuals who fail to respond properly and quickly to the continual ecosystemic changes associated with the learning processes, as we shall note in future chapters.

Students and their teachers discuss at length the roles of heredity and environment. In order to place each in its proper perspective, I employ the following example. Let us assume we have an intricate, expensive pipe organ composed of four manual keyboards and thousands of pipes with a myriad of stops. This organ has been inherited through chromosomes from our forefathers, who built the organ well. This is the instrument we play throughout life, and it represents ourselves. But this mammoth, intricate, and exquisitely sensitive instrument responds to our ecosystems through the fingers of our senses and the mediation of our brain. The music which issues from this complex organ can be tender, sweet, foreboding, or violent. Its response depends on the ways in which one's ecosystem stimulates it. So we are sensitive instruments that reflect the ways our environments act upon our highly intricate biological systems.

> The silent organ loudest chants
> The Master's requiem.
> —Emerson

Roles of the Five Afferent Tracts

An individual becomes aware of the many ecosystemic changes through the five afferent neural tracts which supply the brain with information. Conversely, a computer cannot function unless it is supplied with proper data from an outside source.

Recapitulating, the first cranial nerve (olfactory) is concerned with the sense of smell. It can tell you when your wife happens to be burning your breakfast toast. But the sense of smell, closely coupled with that of taste (involving the fifth, seventh, and ninth cranial nerves), also functions in the process of learning. Taste and smell are used almost exclusively by infants, along with puppies, whom you've observed to put just about every available object in their mouths, mainly, it appears to me, to better acquaint themselves with their particular environments. Each object has its smell and taste characteristics. Should you doubt this assertion, recall if you can, your own security blanket which you cherished from the time you were an infant. It had its own smell, feel, and taste.

As a matter of fact, these afferent avenues to the brain were the only available ones possessed by the remarkable Helen Keller. She tasted, smelled, and felt her way through life with amazing and remarkable success, because she was both blind and deaf.

These latter two perceptive avenues luckily happen to be available to normal individuals. They learn mainly from what they see (second cranial nerve, the optic) and hear (auditory branch of the eighth cranial nerve). Practically all school knowledge is obtained from these two sensory sources, although the Montessori method has added the sense of touch, arising from the afferent spinal tracts, which supply the brain with this important sensation.

One could hardly play a piano or operate a typewriter properly without the sense of touch, which is also employed by the blind to read Braille. In such a situation, the blind person is substituting a properly working sensory tract (touch) to take the place of their inoperable optic neural pathways. This same approach is employed by therapists who teach the deaf to lip read or to observe hand symbols (via their normally functioning optic tracts) so as to understand what others are conveying to them.

5

The Cortical
Brain Centers

Did you ever ask children to think? Usually, they look at you as though you have "flipped your lid." They don't know what to do—laugh, shout, or dance! Can you explain to others what thinking consists of? When you ask a child to think, I believe you really wish him to recall some information he has already learned.

This term of thinking is highly elusive. I dislike using it because very few people really can explain what it is supposed to mean or imply. I prefer the term *cerebration*—the use of all the brain functions that are known. These functions consist of the perception of data from one's environment, its deposit or storage, its proper recall (remembering), and its interpretation or correlation. We shall consider various aspects of these highly important cerebral functions in this chapter.

In the previous chapter we discussed the five important sensory tracts which were involved in bringing ecosystemic information to the brain. After this data, in the form of neural energy, arrives in the proper receptive brain areas, certain lesser known neuroelectrochemical changes occur in these various brain centers. Changes in the brain cells take place. We shall describe some of these. Research, involving this phase of learning, is progressing at a rapid rate, but much more knowledge must be obtained before we can actually know how learning takes place.

Of the many current psychological theories of learning,

few are concerned with what takes place in the brain when learning occurs. Most psychologic theories of learning are concerned with stimulus and its response (S→R theories) and let the subject go at that. However, the neural sciences have come to the rescue, and their important contributions are beginning to shed some light on the actual process of learning.

Theories of Learning

Psychologists and psychiatrists are interested in studying the impairment of brain function, as to orientation, memory, comprehension, calculation, knowledge, learning, judgment, intensity of thought, and quality of affect.

Certain clinical tests are employed to sample the various aspects of the patient's brain function. Cerebral abilities or their lack are directly related to what knowledge an individual was able to store in his cerebral archives, upon what he has learned and how he makes use of it.

As Hilgard (1) has written, so much of an individual's behavior results from learning that some sort of learning theory is essential for understanding and modifying behavior. Hence, we now review various learning theories, and compare them with the Immunologic approach.

At times the phenomena of learning and memory (2) have been linked together. I believe this to be misleading. Later on, we intend to show that though one is dependent upon the other, they are not the same phenomenon.

Morgan (3) defined learning as any relatively constant change of behavior due to past experience. Those changes resulting from the maturation of an individual are to be ruled out.

From the Immunologic approach, we may define learning as those (cortical) brain changes which result from the recording of incoming neural stimuli arising from one's environment. As has been stressed, the main sources of learning are the neural stimuli operable via one or all five afferent pathways to the cerebral cortex. Once such stimuli have arrived, they create neurochemical changes in the various cortical centers. Associated neural pathways interlink these various cortical centers. These neurochemical cortical changes are retained by the process we term *memory*.

Ruch (4) mentions the undesirable learning which may well accompany desirable learning. He calls attention to the child who has a "temper tantrum" while learning, or the child who plays wrong notes while learning to play the piano.

We have observed such experiences in others and perhaps even within ourselves. However, Ruch appears to have confused the nature of the learning stimuli which bombard the cortical receptive centers. We can venture to state that the so-called undesirable evidences of learning have become mixed with desirable aspects. The current trend in psychology is I believe, merely to recognize the learning stimuli and not the *size* of the stimuli. Are these of such strength and quantity as will overwhelm the recipient cortical centers? If so, then those centers will become *hyper*sensitized, or, as Hull stated, receive overlearning, and the efferent neural responses will be pathologic; that is, the child will show "temper tantrums" or other undesirable affects.

Some psychologists might make the serious mistake of not measuring and further analyzing the incoming neural (learning) stimuli that affect their recipient cortical centers. There is no differentiation in the fact that such afferent stimuli can either sensitize or hypersensitize such centers. If these learning stimuli are excessive, they can *hyper*sensitize such recording centers. But, if such stimuli are of normal character (dosage), and the perceptive neural avenues are patent and normally functioning, then only a normal response is to be expected.

So again we note that the old behavioristic approach of stimulus→response leaves much to be desired. We must know the amount and the nature of the stimuli which will bombard the cerebral cortical recipient centers to determine what type of learning will result. If these incoming stimuli are excessive, then hypersensitization may result. If such incoming stimuli are normal in amount and character and if all neural structures are functioning properly, then we may assume the resultant learning will be normal.

As with immunologic reactions, a latent period may ensue because of overstimulation to immunogens. Also in the case of learning, a child might well become reticent if *hyper*stimulated by excessive sensory stimuli. In other words, such a hypersensitized child is unable to learn satisfactorily.

The question of one's threshold to excessive neural afferent stimuli also arises. For example, in a factory, when a person encounters excessive and continual noise, he becomes irritated by it. But as time passes, he might become accustomed to the din: he becomes refractory to the excessive neural stimuli. The same type of psychologic reaction can take place whenever an individual becomes overwhelmed by almost any type of stimuli. Thus, excessive perceptual stimuli can produce a refractory state and little if any learning can take place. The hypersensitized individual will then exhibit "temper tantrums" or other forms of abnormal behavior. Such reactions are expressed by the motor and autonomic functions of the neural apparatus. But they are dependent upon those cerebral centers which have become hypersensitized.

How can one test for knowledge amassed as the result of learning? One can use the time honored quiz systems which are employed routinely in most schools. But how can these immunologic (hypersensitized) states be detected? Word association tests together with changes in the psychogalvanic readings, increased polygraphic tracings, etc. are used routinely to pinpoint such hypersensitized states which are termed psychologic complexes by Freudians.

The Leyden Jar Principle

I have had several sad experiences with electricity. During my course in physiology, I prevailed upon my professor to place electrodes on my skull because I believed that the cortical cells manufactured electrical potentials which I was studying with the electrocardiogram and Einthoven triangles of electrical force. This took place in 1925. Although the oscillograph seemed to respond, this attempt to prove the presence of cortical potentials (EEG) was abandoned because the professor doubted my veracity. This painful experience took place about five years before Berger published his famed findings on the electroencephalogram.

Again, during the Blitz of Britain, I constructed a series of Leyden Jars (battery) to manufacture "artificial lightning" to be employed for destroying Nazi aircraft. This plan was given to the Canadian Inventors' Council. I had accidentally set fire to my garage as I tested this apparatus, which later caused the destruction of some Nazi aircraft.

The Leyden jar is a fascinating piece of electrical equipment. It consists of a glass jar which is partially covered (about 2/3 of its lower surface) with either tinfoil or some other conducting metal substance. This allows for its collection of static electricity, since it has a knobbed conductor which connects both the inside and the outside of the jar. This equipment is able to store electrical charges temporarily. It was accidentally discovered by Van Musschenbroeck (5) of the University of Leyden in 1745.

This jar stores static electricity and, when it is touched, discharges an observable shaft of electricity. The human can also act as a Leyden jar, for during cold weather and upon movement, such as rubbing one's feet on a thick rug, he can generate enough static electricity to produce a snapping shock when he touches metal.

Using the above mechanisms, we can infer that the learning (encoding) process operates analogously. The psychoimmunogens (perceptive stimuli) are changed to neural impulses which travel to the recipient cortical centers of the brain where some as yet unknown electroneurochemical changes take place. These are stored in such brain centers, according to the so-called library theory.

These electroneurochemical brain changes can be either normal or abnormal in caliber, depending upon the amount or the doses of the incoming neural afferent stimuli. Certain additional associated afferent stimuli can cause these various centers to discharge if the cortical cells become supercharged with these excessive potentials. If the cortical discharge travels into the efferent (motor) pathways through the motor trunks and to certain muscles, then muscular movements take place. If the Leyden Jar-like cortical discharges spread to associated cortical centers, then various nousic (6) phenomena may take place, such as day-dreaming, dreaming while asleep, fantasy states, etc.

Should the Leyden jar-like discharge travel through the autonomic nervous system, blushing or the blanching of one's skin might occur. These cortical discharges are capable of travel in any or all avenues of exit, as we have mentioned above, and also to other associated cortical areas.

To facilitate the understanding of how our theory explains the process concerning the storage of information in neuroelectrochemical changes, let us use television as a conceptual model. The transmission of perceptive electrochemical impulses can be regarded as being somewhat similar to the transmission of images via television, by a transformation of visual and auditory activity to electronic impulses that are received by the TV set in the home and reconstituted as visual and auditory activity.

With the case of one's neural perceptive stimulations to the brain, derived from one or more of the five human senses, such neural stimuli travel to the recipient cortical cerebral centers where they are stored as mentioned with the functioning of the Leyden jar principle. These stored

electrochemical potentials have been recorded by the electroencephalogram, and these potentials change with various
situations such as learning. Among these situations the
sleeping and the waking state and, of greater importance,
the various forms of epilepsy. It should be held in mind that
the state of functioning is highly important; for, if a break in
the circuitry takes place, the involved circuit cannot function
properly.

Let us now consider how others feel about this process of
learning. Perhaps one of the outstanding modern contrib-
utors in this respect is Professor D. O. Hebb (7), who most
succinctly observed that we have quite a way to travel before
the principles of behavior are understood to the degree that
the principles of chemical reaction are understood. We
might comment that behavior will be understood much
better just as soon as the principles of the intimate chemical
reactions are known which take place within and without
(intra and extracellular) the cortical cells, which are changed
neurochemically by the neural stimuli that bombard them.

As Hebb wrote (8), almost any current theory concerning
behavior must be inadequate and incomplete. The immunologic approach may be of help toward discovering how the
brain controls behavior.

Hebb (9) mentions that psychology has failed to explain
satisfactorily the process of thought or the inability of neurophysiology to explain cortical transmission. He feels these
points demonstrate the weaknesses of modern psychologic
theory. He points out that the process of thinking inter-
venes between the interactions which take place between the
sensory (incoming) neural impulses and the (outgoing)
motor responses. These central processes seem to be enshrouded in mystery. We now believe that the Immunologic
approach may open the door to understanding such
phenomena.

Hebb (10) wrote about a phase sequence which was a
"thought process," and was dependent upon the interaction

of various portions of the cerebral cortex. He wrote of "the prototype of attention" where "each assembly action might be aroused by its action on the preceding assembly." This is the association of ideas which has been described for many years by many investigators. Hebb mentioned Humphrey's concern about this direction of thought, which he feels is necessary to adult waking behavior. According to this same author, he regards such cortical organization as a form of connectionism, or another variety of the "switchboard" type of behavior.

Hebb is most remarkable in presenting highly interesting ideas and concepts which serve as specific items for further discussion. For example, Hebb (11) wrote that he became perplexed as to how it was "possible for a man to have an I.Q. of 160 or higher after a pre-frontal lobe had been removed, or for a woman...to have an I.Q. of 115...after losing the entire right half of the cortex." We might explain that both of these patients each had two eyes and two ears which we assume were functioning properly prior to their surgical bouts. In the interim before surgery, each had been able to sensitize *both sides of the cerebri*. They were able to learn. So when one side was destroyed or inactivated because of surgery, the other side was capable of functioning. However, we should append that the matter of cerebral dominance might enter our discussion if we would wish to be a bit more specific.

The Matter of Set

Now we arrive at a most intriguing problem which has baffled psychologists throughout these many years. Hebb (12) has called this phenomenon the "autonomous central process." Other terms for this same observation include set, purpose, insight, attention, attitude, need, vector, preoccupation, preservation, expectancy, and hypothesis. As Hebb defined this phenomenon it involves "the recognition that responses are determined by something else besides the immediately preceding sensory stimulation." Hebb feels that "set" doesn't deny the importance of an immediate stimulation, but he rejects the notion that the matter of sensory stimulus is the ultra in behavior. He mentioned Hull's observation concerning this "stimulus trace" which consists of a lasting cerebral state which is "set up" by a specific stimulus, but it isn't transmitted or abolished at once. This peculiar state apparently exerts some sort of an effect on behavior but it isn't a portion of the current afferent stimulus.

Hebb focuses attention on the assumption that neural excitation by itself does not describe or explain "Set." Neural pathways are important so far as their function is concerned, which consists of transmitting neural impulses. The usually accepted concept that neural pathways explain total behavior is, in reality, quite absurd, for such a concept leaves out brain functioning. Such an important and complex organ as the brain should certainly not be disregarded or overlooked, even if its many functions are not understood.

To us at least, "set" is directly dependent upon past learning; that is upon the results from the previous many afferent excitations which have bombarded and further sensitized the recipient groups of nerve cells in the cerebrum. Such results, connected with the actual learning processes, are stored in consequence the neurobiochemical changes to which we have referred from time to time. This storage of these changed former neural impulses really constitutes one's capacity for memory. They are stored at least semipermanently as the Leyden jar can store static electrical currents.

When a related psychoimmunogen (neural afferent stimulus) transmits its resultant neural impulse, it is carried via its afferent trunk (hearing, seeing, feeling, smelling, or tasting) to its recipient storage centers on both sides of the individual's brain (unless one or more sensoria are inoperative).

Thus the receiving brain centers, which have been sensitized by previous associated stimuli, now recognize these similar stimuli. Depending upon the size of the incoming stimuli and the current state of the recipient cortical cells (due to previous learning), plus the length of time which has passed since such sensitizing processes, a *refractory state* might well ensue. This sensitizing process seems to resemble the identical phenomenon observed in allergic states. This is the refractory phase we referred to previously.

Many clinical examples can be cited to demonstrate such a process. For instance, we speak of becoming speechless when a person is confronted with an overwhelming dose of associated psychoimmunogens (psychoantigens) which bombard a previously sensitized cerebral area.

We know that a caged rabbit, when placed adjacent to a caged snake, can become so markedly overwrought as to cause the rabbit's death! The chicken whose head is held so that its eyes follow a chalk line will remain standing in a motionless state resembling a trance. This phenomenon might well be similar to the hypnotic trance experienced by a hypnotized human subject.

We should explain that the chalk-line phenomenon might be associated with the shape of a snake, i.e., a long, thin chalk line. When the chicken sees this, it becomes hypersensitized to the concept of an actual snake. Some of these psychoimmunologic residual concepts appear to be inherited. Why will a king snake immediately attack and kill a rattler if such an inherited state were not present? Or why does a red squirrel attack a grey squirrel and cause the latter to become castrated? These are so-called instincts which Mother Nature has endowed in her scheme for living fauna and flora.

So we can discover that this so-called "set" can be either inherited, acquired, or both. It is produced also whenever a psychoimmunogen (psychoantigen) produces a stimulus which is related to the results from inheritance or previous sensitizations in the recipient cortical cells.

A similar state occurs whenever two fighting cocks are pitted against each other. As soon as they see each other, they stand motionless until they become motivated to do battle from possibly an outpouring of adrenalin or other humoral and glandular substances caused by viewing their adversary. The initial psychoimmunologic shock from such sight produces a temporary refractory state, during which time they remain motionless for various periods of time. Such refractory states are usually shortened by throwing the cocks towards each other, which incidentally makes our own "blood boil" with resentment from such barbaric procedures as practiced by humans who should know better!

Perhaps the refractory state produced by intense fright in some animals and birds allow for their capture by predatory creatures. Such a refractory state can produce a "freezing" response when the captive animal is unable to flee to safety. These might be easily explained when we know more about the chemistry of the brain.

Various Aspects of Learning

We have made the point that "set" might well be closely associated with the refractory period characteristic of allergic states. Allergists agree with the psychologists that such a state exists, but neither group of scientists knows much concerning the patho-physiologic events connected with such a phenomenon, which might be a temporary state of biologic shock resulting from the induction of allergens and/or psychoimmunogens. This phenomenon is open to more needed research in both fields.

It is well at this time to mention again our theory model of the Leyden jar as exemplified by the various cortical cell centers which store the results of previous sensitizing reactions. The storage is learning and the product of the storage is knowledge. The individual has been sensitized to the Gestalt of his surroundings in the form of neurochemical-electrical changes which are stored in these cortical centers.

When one studies the neural anatomy and the physiology of these various cortical centers, it will be observed that various intricate neural connections exist; some have been minutely traced between such cortical centers. These neural connecting pathways have to do with the phenomenon of association. One cortical area, being intimately connected with other associated areas, upon stimulation, can produce associated stimulation in other various cortical areas. Thus, when one smells a rose, he might think of the thorns which he remembers (having been traumatized before by these prickers) as he smelled the aroma of the rose. Obviously, these associated areas were sensitized concomitantly as he smelled the flower (olfactory tract). He also probably observed the color of the rose, its red or yellow (perception via the optic tracts). So upon subsequent stimulations by the psychoimmunogen, in this case the flower, he might also recall readily any of the previous associated sensitizations. All this to do with memory, its association tracts, and its chemistry.

Obviously, if any nerve tracts or their recording (storage) centers happen to be rendered inactive because of disease or trauma, such afferent and efferent routes are impaired or obliterated, according to the tenets of our theory.

The discharging associated cortical cells (resembling the discharge of a charged Leyden jar) cause awareness or the state of consciousness. The individual perceives the effects from these various discharges of the various associated cortical cells and their centers as they react to other incoming neural stimuli from the many psychoimmunogens (psycho-antigens) in the individual's environment. He reacts more to some psychoimmunologic stimulations than he does to others because of his previous sensitizations (learning). He then focuses on these points of interest or on those psychoimmunogens which might even challenge his welfare (defense reaction).

Should such a rapport be broken, then sensory frustration results. (More will be said about such frustrating reactions later on.) But if this perceptual interplay is allowed to continue uninterrupted, the individual either learns (stores the neurochemical results from the sensitization of these recipient cortical cells) or his cortical centers discharge and send impulses to the autonomic or motor systems. Hence the individual blushes, runs, or even fights.

And plausibly with schizophrenics, their hypersensitized cortical cells (recalling the Leyden jar principle where this jar becomes supercharged) might discharge at random. These indiscriminate volleys from the various supersensitized cortical cells, resulting from overlearning, might well produce the many bizarre aspects of behavior as often witnessed with such unpredictable mental patients. We will have more to relate on these abnormal aspects of human behavior in another chapter, when both the nousic and the histic aspects of such abnormal behavior will be discussed.

A prevailing psychologic idea was that the central nervous system has little function except to convey sensory neural impulses finally to the autonomic and motor systems. However, this hypothesis has been shown to be faulty; as Hebb (13) commented, this concept of "sensory dominance" still prevails among many current psychologists.

Hebb stresses the concept that quick learning in an adult will occur when a neural stimulation produces what he calls "well organized phase sequences" (14). We believe what Hebb was stressing is, to use our theoretical approach, that quick learning in the adult cannot occur unless an associated psychoimmunogen's neural stimulations react upon the recipient's previously sensitized cortical areas, which had become sensitized through similar neurochemical changes.

From these previously sensitized cortical areas evolves the clue as to what recognition is physiologically. Attention is closely associated with it. However, recognition consists of an afferent stimulus (psychoimmunogen or psychoantigen) which meets with a state of sensitization, in itself specific, in the recipient cortical cells. If the new stimulation is of sufficient strength or caliber, a further cortical sensitization may occur. Hence, finally hypersensitization may be produced, thereby setting off the first appearance of abnormal behavior. Hebb alludes to such a concept, although he does not use immunologic principles for his explanations of "set," which Hull attempted to define with his "oscillation principle" (15). Hebb made a point of mentioning the rational basis for the serious consideration of a "central factor" which can modify the neurophysiologic results from neural stimuli. He made another highly important statement when he stressed that it is necessary for psychologists to discover new concepts which are physiologically sound in order to consider the many complexities of central neural action (16). He further pointed out that the real significance of synaptic connections should be reexamined. On the subjects of learning and memory, Hebb further observed that he found it "hard to understand how repeated sensations can reinforce one another, with the lasting effect we call learning and memory" (17). We believe that we have explained how repeated sensitizations from related psychoallergens produce the phenomena of memory and learning.

Hull's theory for learning, as quoted by Hebb (18), was that learning took place through "constant causal relationships between stimulus, intervening variables and response." What Hull alluded to was the use of stimulus, perhaps followed by cortical function, which finally led to response (motor aspect). Again, Hull's concept finds itself in accord with the Psychoimmunologic theory, but the "cortical function" portion of his theory does not explain how stimuli affect the recipient cortical cells, leading eventually to the subject's response, whatever it might be.

Again, Hebb (19) has commented that adult learning

seems to involve the use of combinations of familiar patterns and perceptions. Learning is helped by employing already familiar names and events. In other words, Hebb employed the sensitizing and the storage of those changes in recipient cortical cells to further added learning procedures. This reasoning is in complete agreement with the Psychoimmunologic Theory.

The paucity of sufficient scientific data as to what happens between stimulation and response has been cited by Kohler (20). He mentioned the necessity of inventing hypotheses concerning what possibly happens within the organism, since its interior is not accessible presently to observation. He felt these interpretations regarding what he termed the "terra incognita" was about the most important subject of all to be understood.

This lack of a logical, scientific hypothesis for such interval functions of the individual is observed with most psychologic attempts at explaining behavior; and, as we have stated, this constitutes the *raison d'etre* for our current reflections.

Ruch (21) stated that learning is concerned with certain changes in the individual's nervous system; however, such changes were not identified, because the process of learning had to be observed indirectly as responses of the individual to stimuli. Such changes cause modification in the individual's behavior, which must be controlled to rule out certain variables. He noted that conditioning was a fundamental type of learning, in which the individual learns to respond to wide varieties of stimulus situations. He wrote about the apparent difference between instrumental and classical conditioning, which he stated were separated as follows: With classical conditioning, the unconditioned stimulus and the conditioned stimulus are used jointly. The conditioning result tends to use these two types of stimuli to obtain a particular response already obtained in behavioral learning. With instrumental conditioning, no eliciting stimuli are employed, since the subject of the experiment is placed in some sort of an experimental situation where an instrumental response occurs with the reinforcement by reward (22). Ruch also described other forms for learning such as motor learning, verbal learning, perceptual learning, attitude learning, and problem solving. Our readers are referred to Ruch's textbook for added details on these types of learning.

Let us suspend our review of the so-called behavioristic school on the matter of learning to interject a few comments which now come to our attention. From what we have already learned from the psychoimmunologic theory, it seems obvious enough that placing an animal in an experimental situation, say a maze, will not yield well-controlled behavioral responses if the animal is supposed to run the maze. In this particular situation, he uses his eyesight for learning purposes. But what of the other four avenues of perception which he might use for learning if these are not closed, at least temporarily, during the entire experiment?

If not shut off by one device or another, the dog will be able to perceive a scent in case the maze was not cleaned properly before the experiment. His cortical centers will pick up auditory impulses (leads) if the experimenter and his staff speak during such an experiment. The dog may even use his powers for proprioception if these receptors aren't controlled properly, and his taste perceptions will possibly upset the proper results of this experiment if not controlled properly. So we should realize that each and every avenue of perception must be controlled as well as such currently unappreciated controls as to the size, duration, and caliber of stimuli, plus the time factors, which can easily upset one's proper experimental findings if not controlled properly. We wish to emphasize that, with any one or more of the experimental animals, five avenues for perception must be accounted for before an experiment is controlled properly. The reason for this is to make certain that the experimental animal learns only through the sensory avenue or avenues chosen for such an experiment. Any animal can learn through one or more avenues of perception if these afferent stimuli can travel over physiologically normal functioning pathways where such impulses are recorded in the animals' cerebral archives. And what should be done about the results of the many previous sensitizations which the animal has stored in his cortical areas of association? How can these be controlled adequately?

Kimble (23) observed that learning produced a relatively permanent behavioral change because of practice. He wrote that the salivary responses to Pavlovian conditioning were the very simplest forms of learning. Kimble made the following observations on this so-called simple form of learning which was based upon a typical Pavlovian experiment. This consisted of a dog as the experimental subject. A tone would be heard by the dog for several seconds, and then some meat was fed to the dog. Following several of such paired stimulations, salivation occurred in the dog at the sound of the auditory stimulus by hearing the tone. Thus, the introduction of the tone evoked a response which had been produced solely by seeing or eating the meat.

Four basic items were involved in this conditioning process, namely (1) the conditioned simulus which produced no response at the outset of the experiment, in this case the tone. (2) The unconditioned stimulus produced a normal response with the use of meat in this experiment. The unconditioned response was salivation. The conditioned response resulted when both the unconditioned stimulus and the conditioned stimulus are introduced together.

In psychoimmunologic terms, obviously the dog's cerebral cells had been sensitized to the previous sight and taste of meat. The use of a tone further sensitized associated cerebral areas which received the auditory impulses. Thus an association was formed, and the further sensitization (psychoimmunogenization) of such sensitized cortical areas produced Leyden-jar-like neural discharges which entered the dog's autonomic and motor systems. Thus salivation occurred. Instrumental conditioning can be understood in psychoimmunologic terms through the use of similar theoretical principles of Psychoimmunology.

A rather commonly observed clinical example will stress our view of *immediate* learning in contrast to the Pavlovian concept. A huge dose of psychoimmunogens in a very short time is capable of producing lifelong changes in behavior as the result of such powerful and rapid cerebral hypersensitizations. For instance, a mother sees her child run over by the car her husband, and the father of their child, happens to be driving. The mother hereafter will no doubt react everytime she sees a driveway or when she hears or reads about a similar happening. This one intense period of hypersensitization was sufficient to change her behavior possibly for the rest of her life. This is the stuff which furnished the Freudian school with ammunition. However, it can be explained readily and sufficiently by use of the psychoimmunologic principles, since any psychoimmunogen, associated in any way with the above accident, can recall such a painful incident not only to the mother but also to anyone who happened to be present at the unfortunate scene.

Had the mother experienced a previous similar psychoimmunologic response, and then had a similar additional painful episode become superimposed upon her previous sensitizations, we would certainly expect a hypersensitization process to occur. This might induce a form of serious emotional upheaval wherein she might scream, tear her hair, and become manic. So we can note that a previous allied sensitization (cortical) process must be taken into account, plus the time factors and the size or caliber of the psychoimmunogens (psychoantigens) which have played upon the sensoria of the individual. Her response will be directly dependent upon the exact nature and the scope of these total cerebral neurochemical changes fashioned by these associated psychoimmunogens and possible similar episodes she might have experienced previously.

Kimble (24) stated that intelligence could be influenced by experience. We doubt this, because we believe intelligence is directly associated with any individual's ability to form psychoimmunologic states from the introduction of psycho-immunogens (learning). Such states can be considered as either of normal or abnormal intensity, depending upon the variables we have mentioned before. We further assert that one's intelligence is connected directly with his innate cerebral equipment, which is associated with heriditary factors to a considerable extent. If he inherited a sound cerebral system and all afferent and efferent pathways are intact and are operating normally, he will cerebrate, that is, employ the stored psychoimmunologic states, as does an intelligent and rational person. He might be substandard, normal, or brilliant depending upon all of the above variant factors which have to do with his nousic capabilities.

Morgan (25) wrote that forgetting and remembering are merely opposites. The amount of forgetting is really the difference between the amount learned and that which is retained. We regard remembering as the ability to use those psychoimmunogized and stored potentials in the cortical learning areas when desired, which is known as recall. Forgetting consists of the partial or complete loss of these cortical neurochemical potentials which have resulted from learning from various environmental psychoimmunogens.

Recall also makes use, we believe, of the stored cortical potentials (the Leyden jar principle) via the various neural connections between these charged or supercharged cortical areas. The various associated neural tracts transport these releases of energy from the various sensitized or super-sensitized cortical areas that had been energized by previous psychoimmunologic sensitization. Thus, the various word association tests and the other diagnostic psychologic and psychiatric mechanisms can test either the presence or the

absence of such cortical sensitizations or hypersensitizations.

As pointed out by Morgan (25) (26), most contemporary
psychologists employ various theories to explain certain observations. Perhaps the reason for the use of one or multiple
theories to explain certain aspects of behavior lies with the
situation that none of these theories is capable of doing the
explaining well enough by itself. However, we believe that
our theory is fundamental enough for such purposes, since it
employs only a biologically oriented approach which, so far
at least, has not varied with the passage of time nor the
coming or the going of various other psychologic theories.
These have waned in their popularity and with their various
adherents, the current beliefs of their supporters. Like "Ole
Man River" the Psychoimmunologic Theory "jest goes
rollin' on" for well over some thirty years without any necessary basic revisions.

Compare Hull's forty-two variables, used in his theory of
learning, to our basic concepts and you will note the simplicity of our approach. In this same context, Hilgard (27)
mentioned that what we call learning might be a function of
nervous tissue. Where does such learning happen? Is it in
the nerve tracts, the various or certain parts of the brain, or
in the efferent nerve components? Obviously, we assume it
takes place in those cortical centers that have been changed
neurochemically by the afferent nerve impulses (forms of
energy) bombarding the centers.

Hilgard (28) proposed some pertinent questions about
learning which an adequate theory should be able to answer.
This situation reminds us of Don Quixote's brave but rather
foolhardy charge at the windmill as we gird ourselves to face
and question some current psychologic wisdom regarding
the topic of learning!

1. *What are the limits of learning?*

To date, our discussion has mentioned such important
factors as the size of the perceptual stimuli, the all-important

time factor, the nature of the recording and storage centers and other variables, not to overlook maturation (age) and the hereditary advantages or disadvantages which endow each individual. Obviously, the question resolves itself to the matter of individual differences, which will vary with each individual since no two are identical. Hence, all variants will be observed, according to the norm curve, when the ability to learn is considered. Obviously, there will be all types of variance in such abilities as are inherent to the species involved; that is, in the degree to which the capability for normal psychoimmunologic states can emerge.

2. *What is the role of practice in learning?*

The answer to this question should be crystal clear. Practice involves reinforcement, which is the further introduction of related afferent stimuli whose sensitizing results are stored in their related cerebral cell centers. However, that fragile dividing line which separates the normal sensitizing cortical processes from the abnormal hypersensitizing states is currently unknown. Again, we suggest that the limits for each of these states is a matter of individual differences, which can be divided further into those factors we have discussed previously. To summarize our answers to the questions raised, practice (reinforcement) can assist the process of learning to a certain normal limit. If this limit is exceeded ed, neurotic or psychotic events might occur as the result of hypersensitization (overlearning due to overstimulation from related psychoimmunogens.)

3. *How important are drives and incentive, rewards and punishments?*

As Hilgard suggests, it is easier to learn interesting rather than dull things. The effects from interesting afferent stimuli work better than do the uninteresting ones, which might introduce some injury (painful stimuli) capable of hypersensitizing the recipient cortical centers. Thus, by the same token, rewards and punishments are not equal, since rewards tend to reinforce the effects from learning, whereas

punishments can be dangerous because of possible hypersensitizations from noxious afferent stimuli that can produce
pain. We think the outcome depends heavily on the dosage
and the type of psychoallergens which are perceived, plus
the previous experiences (sensitizations) of each individual.

4. *What is the place of understanding and insight?*

Reinforcement of the effects from former learning (reinforcing psychogenic effects) helps the learning process, that
is, the storage of knowledge. Some psychoimmunogens
(symbols) function only if the C.N.S. effects from previous
sensitizations (learning) are related neurochemically in the
recipient brain cells so that recognition and the ensuing reinforcement can take place. It follows that learning entirely
new symbols is much more difficult than learning those symbols which were related to former learning situations. With
new symbols or afferent stimuli, the cortical cell sensitizations have to begin from scratch. With recognizable psychoimmunologic reinforcement, the learning process proceeds
well, unless the dosage happens to be huge and overwhelming enough to produce hypersensitization.

5. *Does learning one thing help you learn something else?*

Yes, this is true if the afferent stimuli are related so their
cortical effects mesh with those areas of association which
have been sensitized by previous related psychoimmunogens. The above holds true only if the dosage and the time
periods produce sensitization in the recipient cortical areas.

6. *What happens when we remember and when we
forget?*

Such situations have been explained fully previously by
the psychoimmunologic theory. When comparing the
various cognitive theories with the several stimulus—
response theories, the main differences encountered are
produced by differences in interpretation, according to
Hilgard (29). Ideas that have been experienced simultaneously are associated. From our viewpoint, several or more
neural centers become sensitized from the same afferent

stimuli. These cortical centers (brain and spinal cord) are intimately connected by neural tracts of association. Hence, when one center later reacts to an associated psychoimmunogen, the other sensitized areas will also respond neurochemically. We could term such responses as being of a sympathetic nature. For example, if a child sees a dog that is barking vehemently, he becomes sensitized by at least two perceptive routes—the visual and the auditory tracts. If the dog attacks the child during this first encounter and bites the child, then the (touch and pain) afferent avenues sensitize also those cortical centers they supply. Also, if the child feels the hot breath of the attacking dog, more sensitizations can occur, and the olfactory pathway can enhance the primary sensitizations of the victim (child). If such an attack is painful, the chances are the child will become hypersensitized to the same dog through four of the five perceptive avenues if they happen to be patent. Henceforth, the sight of the dog or even the dog's barking will produce a response from the sensitized child's cortical centers, depending upon the state of these sensitizations or hypersensitizations. However, the time factor becomes important, since the passage of time can cause these psychoimmunogized states to lose some of their stored energy.

John (30) distinguished the main difference between learning and memory as "read-in" with the former and "read-out" with the latter subject. We might append the concept of the Leyden jar principle, in that learning is the storage of energy in the form of neurochemical sensitizing changes in the recipient cortical cells. Memory would be the discharge (probably only partial) of these energized neurochemical states to and from the various cortical association areas. Such discharges are often shunted into the efferent neural systems, such as the motor and the autonomic systems, which respond histically to such outgoing neural impulses, exemplified by screaming, fainting, etc. RNA, or ribonucleic acid, as synthesized in the brain cell areas, is possibly one of the energy forms which exists as the result of neural sensitizations. It is believed that RNA increases with neural stimulation of these cortical areas, as do proteins following learning. Learning is interfered with if the synthesis of RNA is impeded, and more rapid learning occurs with the speeding up of RNA manufacture.

John calls attention to the role of puromycin which can interfere with the synthesis of protein, but RNA formation is not involved with the use of puromycin. We are just beginning to understand some aspects of the neurochemistry of the brain, as exemplified also by Humphrey and Coxon's (31) volume.

Mitchell, Beaton, and Bradley (32) wrote: "No one knows what changes take place in the brain when an organism acquires information; nor is it known how this information, once stored, is retrieved and acted upon. What is known is that there exists lawful relationships between an organism's past history and its subsequent behavior. What are known are some empirical rules of thumb for manipulating, for modifying behavior, and the overwhelming majority of work on learning thus far has addressed itself to the elucidation of these lawful relationships; to behavior, its description, its quantification (where possible), and the elaboration of the contingencies which affect it. Relatively little work has been done on the underlying physiological substrate of learning."

These same investigators state that a RNA mediator hypothesis is "hardly compelling" since the brain extracts that contain RNA also have other macromolecules, such as polysaccharides, proteins, glycoproteins, and polypeptides. To date, no one has been able to obtain a transfer effect with only RNA in such a solution.

Mitchell, Beaton, and Bradley feel that polypeptides, found in RNA extracts, might be involved in this transfer phenomenon. Furthermore, they consider that memory may be related to a "permanent alteration of synaptic function." Also, "behavior-specific peptides might provide the explication of information storage and retrieval.''

Smithies (33) considers the brain as being not too different from a large modern computer which has been designed to execute complex functions or a large number of various programs simultaneously. He wrote: ''Besides its basic computing machinery it must have an extensive metaorganizational system. It must analyse and order the incoming programmes, distribute these to the revalent subsections of the computing machinery (which must be switched off when not in use), decide on when to ask for more data, allot priorities to the different programmes, and distribute the elements in these to different types of memory bank as required, and finally omit the one output most adopted to the circumstances.''

6

Subcortical

Areas and

Functions

Although the departments of the neural sciences are only about fifteen years old, hardly a week passes without the publication of new and varied advances in the numerous professional journals. The flow of articles appears endless, since additional information is so necessary to understand the true functioning of many anatomic parts.

Various theories concerned with behavior have their advocates. But basic concepts change as additional evidence supports or detracts from established viewpoints. A recent article by Powers (1) illustrates this point. He writes that "when controlled quantities are discovered, the related stimulus-response laws become trivially predictable. Variability of behavior all but disappears once controlled quantities are known. Behavior itself is seen in terms of this model to be self-determined in a specific and highly significant sense that calls into serious doubt the ultimate feasibility of operant conditioning of human beings by other human beings."

Data which is concerned with psychophysical law has been turned about by evidence derived from neuroelectric findings, according to Stevens (2). Much of such data will be difficult to understand for those readers who have not had advanced courses in the sciences. But such articles will give the reader information as to what is necessary to enter these important scientific fields of research.

Similar divergent arguments which concern various transplants from one animal to another have been graphically recorded in an article containing statements by Bryant, Golub, McConnell, and Rosenblatt, followed by those from Stein and Rosen (3). These opposing views are to be found in many scientific discussions. Perhaps the passage of time will tell which is correct.

The Papez-MacLean Pathways

The cerebral cortex appears to be concerned with highest level neural functioning. It is here that problem solving, the making of decisions, the receipt of afferent neural impulses (producing learning), their storage and retrieval take place. This huge and important structure, complex as it is, can be regarded as the Freudian ego, the pilot for the direction and the behavior the body will follow.

The subcortical structures, such as the thalamus and its subthalamic parts, serve as the centers for emotion producing sensations and for the determination as to whether or not an impulse, coming from the cortex, is pleasurable or painful. Also, these subcortical regions are concerned with life-supporting mechanisms. These inform the cortex when the individual becomes thirsty, hungry, originates sexual urges and emotional reactions.

The cortex and its subcortical structures are connected by the Papez-MacLean neural network, which is highly important in the study of behavior. Both parts, that is, the cortex and the subcortical centers, are supplied with the Papez-MacLean neural fibers which are to send and also receive neural impulses from each component.

For example, a bear sees a supply of honey through his optic tracts. He may also smell this delicacy which supplies information to the bear's cerebral cortex through his olfactory tracts. Neural impulses travel to the bear's sub-cortical nuclei where the feeling of pleasure is formulated and thence returned to the brain. But should the honey contain a bee, which stings the bear's mouth, the animal receives this sensory impulse to the subcortical areas, which quickly interpret the sensation as being painful, returns it to the cortex which rapidly tells the bear to escape or to snap at the painful source. The final behavior, so far as the bear is concerned, is what the subcortical centers tell the bear's brain. If the subcortical sensations remain pleasurable, and without pain, the bear will eat his fill until the subcortical center informs the brain that the bear has had enough honey.

It is important to call the reader's attention to the importance of the neural connections which exist between the cortex, the thalamus, corpus striatum, the reticular network, and the efferent (outgoing) or motor nerve tracts, termed the extrapyramidal system. This bundle of nerves, originating in the cerebral cortex, connects the thalamic areas to the motor neural tract, the extrapyramidal system with the muscles.

Much research has been and is being accomplished in determining the functions of the subcortical centers, since the physiology of these areas has not as yet been established fully. For example, the relationships of the subcortical systems to the brain mechanisms and vision are discussed in a rather recent paper (4).

Davenport and Balagura (5) question the presence of a hunger center in the rat's lateral hypothalamus. Smith, *et al.* (6) believe the lateral hypothalamus has a cholinoceptive mechanism which controls the killing of mice by rats.

DeLong (7) studied the function of the putamen in relation to slow and rapid arm movement in monkeys. He believes the putamen (a part of the basal ganglia) is involved in slow arm movements.

Although I cannot locate the reference, I recall an

important experiment when hostile rats were kept in a cage. They fought frequently. Another cage contained rats which were docile. The thalamic areas of the hostile rats proved to have become much larger than the thalami of the docile rats. This experiment appears to show hypertrophy of the thalami of hostile rats as compared to the lesser used or involved thalami of the docile animals.

There now exists strong evidence of hypothalamic release factors for each anterior pituitary hormone, according to Yen (8). It is known also that the hypothalamus is also connected with other endocrine functions, such as ovulation and the estrous (menstruating) cycles, and might well exert contractions of the intestines through a hormone excreted from the hypothalamus.

Subcortical Relationships

Literature from the many researches conducted by neuroscientists is often contradictory. However, we might summarize the numerous better accepted data as to the roles played by the subcortical centers.

It is believed the intact cerebral cortex inhibits the subcortical centers which produce emotional responses. Removing the cortex experimentally causes all inhibitions to be removed, which allows the subcortical centers to control the individual's further behavior. In other words, the thalamic and hypothalamic regions then control behavior. Without the presence of the cerebral cortex (decorate animal) an uninhibited emotional display can ensue. Other studies have shown the limbic structures inhibit the hypothalamus and that the non-limbic cortex, in turn, modify the inhibiting influences of the limbic system. The removal of the limbic system or combinations of these structures can produce an extremely ferocious animal. However, merely the ablation of the amygdala, a portion of the limbic structure, has produced both placid and ferocious animals.

The subcortical areas, concerned with the production of emotions, are thought to be the limbic cortex, hippocampus, fornix, cingulate, gyrus, the thalamus, mamillary portions of the hypothalamus, the hypothalamus, and also the corpus callosum. Those impulses which produce emotional responses begin in the posterior limbic cortex and pass to the cingulate body which is concerned with the actual production of an emotional display. Stimuli of an intellectual nature, such as thought (cerebration), from the cerebral cortex could involve the limbic cortex, or hypothalamic activity could be transmitted to these structures via the mamillary bodies.

Other investigators believe the hypothalamus integrates and then initiates emotional activities. The limbic system is also involved with visceral responses which can involve the cardiac, circulatory, respiratory, and sweat responses from the eradication or even the stimulation of considerable portions of the limbic apparatus.

Various types of behavior are produced by these subcortical centers. However, the entire system is well integrated and interrelated, and obviously is highly complex. The thalamus receives sensory impulses on their way to the cerebral cortex. Audition and vision are intimately associated, since the former tract (auditory) runs through the lateral geniculate body, which is closely associated with the medial geniculate body that handles vision. That is probably why a person who approaches a railroad crossing and hears the train whistle invariably looks in the direction of the sound.

The cerebral commissures, including the corpus callosum, relay impulses from one cerebral cortex to the other and vice versa. The cerebellum, mainly concerned with proprioception, has nerves to and from the basal ganglia. These, in turn, connect with the medulla, which has to do with respiration and other vital processes.

Although the hypothalamus is about one per cent of the entire brain's weight, it is believed that this small organ is involved with the individual's emotions and motivation. It exhibits a greater supply of blood vessels than any other portion of the subcortical structures. Perhaps hunger and its satiation are triggered by this very important structure because of the blood sugar level changes. The hypothalamus is also very sensitive to bodily temperature changes and to fluid balance fluctuations.

The reticular bodies should be mentioned also, because these appear to be related intimately with the subthalamus. The hippocampus appears to either increase or decrease sexual activity when stimulated. Lesions produced in this structure appear, in man at least, to produce the inability to learn new data. So we can note that the entire subcortical structures are highly complex and, no doubt, will yield more important information with further research.

We now have reached an important stage. Theoretically at least, those neural impulses, originating from one's ecosystem, arrive at the recipient areas of the cerebral cortex. Then some become transmitted to the subcortical areas. Here these stimuli can be interpreted as being either pleasure-producing or pain-producing in nature. If of the pleasurable variety, neural impulses returning to the cerebral cortex will tend to attract the individual to the source of these pleasure-producing stimuli. If pain-producing stimuli from the subcortical centers enter the cerebral cortex, the individual will tend to avoid such noxious sources in his ecosystem. The efferent (motor) neural pathways will respond accordingly, that is, bring the individual (by walking or running) to the pleasure-producing ecosystemic source, or the individual will tend to flee the pain-producing ecosystemic source. In other words, pleasurable stimuli attract, and painful stimuli tend to repel their recipient.

Perhaps this explains why the youngster spies his mother put cookies in a jar on the pantry shelf, and when she leaves, he goes to the source of this pleasure-producing stimuli, puts his hand in the cookie jar, begins to salivate, which is the first portion of the digestive process, and bites into the delectable food. It tastes so good he nearly swallows the entire cookie.

Perhaps the child's mother wishes to establish an adverse reaction in her child with his cookie-snatching tendencies. So she mixes the cookie dough with alum. When the child bites into such a cookie, he obtains a very bitter taste. So he spits out the cookie and avoids further cookie-snatching raids in the pantry because his experience became painful rather than pleasurable.

A young man is attracted to a young, beautiful, and smiling female. But his amorous intentions can become turned off if the girl's mother appears suddenly, or the young female has bad halitosis or body odors. This has been exploited at length by manufacturers in their advertising procedures. Similar neural mechanisms have operated in both situations because of the nature of the subcortical neural impulses which reach the individual's brain, and whether such stimuli have been pain or pleasure-producing will determine their behavior.

Pain sensations can produce frustrations which appear to originate in these subcortical areas. More will appear on the matter of frustratory mechanisms in a subsequent chapter.

7

Efferent

Neural Tracts

Until the present, we have been interested mainly in how an individual receives data from his ecosystem (environment) via the five perceptive neural tracts to the brain where encoding, storage, and retrieval of such data are operable at the subcortical areas. At these centers the individual interprets the cortical impulses mainly as to whether they are painful or pleasurable. These subcortical impulses then are returned to the cerebral cortex where a decision, via cerebration (thinking), is made. Should the individual avoid further painful impulses, or should he become attracted to pleasurable sources for further examination, he proceeds accordingly.

Once a decision is made, he is unable to act properly unless he possesses some means for moving his body to the sources. For example, if a girl sees a beautiful bush, covered by roses, and she becomes stimulated by the floral scent therefrom; her cortical and subcortical centers inform her about this pleasure-producing object, which happens to be the rose bush in this situation. So her cerebral cortex sends forth efferent (away from the brain) impulses which signal her locomotory apparati to move to the rose bush where she can smell the rose aroma, handle the roses, examine the nature of the petals. (Are they healthy or diseased? Do they need spraying? etc.) Perhaps she will pick several roses with their stems to adorn herself. All this behavior is pleasurable in nature, and she enjoys the experience.

Now let us assume that a lowly wasp had entered such a blossom and had secreted itself by hiding in the rose blossom. When the girl smells the beautiful flower, the wasp's reaction will be to protect itself from injury by stinging the intruder's nose and then escaping from its threatening environment. The sting immediately causes pain-producing stimuli which signal the young lady to drop the flower and then immediately escape from her now painful environment by running away. What causes her to be able to leave so promptly? Her cerebral cortex sends out neural impulses to the muscles of her hands and feet which precipitously remove her from the pain-producing environment.

We are now interested in discovering how the cerebral cortex tells the young lady how to escape, which is accomplished through the use of the pyramidal and the extrapyramidal (efferent) pathways which supply the girl's musculature with a signal to escape by running from the painful ecosystem.

The pyramidal system originates in the Betz cells of the cerebral cortex in its motor area. This pyramidal tract then enters the internal capsule (adjacent to the corpus callosum) and travels along the brain stem (pons and medulla) where one portion of the pyramidal tract crosses the brain stem (decussion at the pyramids) and forms the lateral cortico-spinal tract and, finally, supplies mainly the hand muscles. A second portion of the pyramidal system goes medially into the spinal cord; it is called the anterior corticospinal tract and goes to the lumbar area. The third portion of the pyramidal tract, the lateral corticospinal tract, also descends in the lateral part of the spinal cord. We can rightfully state that the name of the corticospinal tracts is the same as the pyramidal tract which forms the three component parts of the corticospinal tracts.

The extrapyramidal system also originates in the Betz cells of the motor areas of the cerebral cortex. While the pyramidal system is excitatory in function, the extrapyramidal system is supposedly inhibiting or relaxing to the musculature it supplies. This network of efferent nerves descends the internal capsule, travels through the medulla and pons, and form several main extrapyramidal pathways—namely the reticulospinal, the lateral corticospinal, the vestibulospinal, and reticulospinal tracts—and terminates in the spinal cord.

The above data merely forms a synopsis of the pyramidal tracts. Specific details should be obtained from neurologic textbooks for information about upper and lower motor neuron lesions etc., which have been summarized so well by Gardner (1). He suggested that a series of levels be employed for studying efferent muscular activity. One can begin with the cerebral cortex, then the basal ganglia, followed by the cerebellum, the reticular bodies, the brain stem, and the spinal cord. Gardner states that the extrapyramidal system contains both excitatory and inhibitory functions, while the pyramidal system functions as an excitatory system. He states that the contralateral cerebral hemisphere controls the limb muscles. At the body's midline the muscles have bilateral control from the brain cortex.

The pyramidal and the extrapyramidal systems should be remembered as supplying the body and its musculature so that movement can occur. Diseases which involve muscular disuse are handled by neurologists, who are highly trained in this field, which includes various malfunctions that involve nerves (2), (3) and the tissues they supply with neural impulses.

Chusid and McDonald (4) have called attention to the fact that it is often difficult to separate the pyramidal from the extrapyramidal system, both anatomically and physiologically. These authors claim that the extrapyramidal system is functional rather than anatomical.

8

The Autonomic

System and

Psychosomatics

Brilliant Alexander Comfort (1) wrote that, in his opinion, disease is caused by biochemistry, bacteria, immunology— "whoever sectioned an emotional trauma?" Similarly, biochemical changes in one's body produce emotions. These are under control of the autonomic nervous system, which operates in a more or less automatic manner. It consists of two main components, the para-sympathetic or the craniosacral, or the sympathetic and thoracolumbar division. Most of the work these two divisions accomplish is carried out below consciousness. Nevertheless, the autonomic nervous system is well integrated with the other portions of the nervous system both in function and structure. Since it is so highly complicated, our readers are referred to more complete informational sources, such as modern neurologic textbooks.

The main purpose of the autonomic nervous system is to maintain the inner body's homeostasis, that is, to keep it constant and as nearly normal as possible. We summarize the anatomy of this great neural system in order to convey some idea of how it operates.

The sympathetic division contains connections to all the spinal nerves. It begins in the cervical (neck) portion and ends in the sacral segment, receiving rami (connections) mostly from the intermediolateral cell column of the spinal cord. These rami form the sympathetic chain and run lateral to the cord on both sides of it. Branches from the sympathetic chain supply the sympathetics of the head. Portions of the sympathetic chain connect with the heart and lung plexuses to supply these organs. One branch from the sympathetic runs via the great splanchnic nerve and the lesser splanchnic nerve to the celiac plexus, which supplies the stomach, liver, pancreas, spleen, adrenal medulla, and small intestines. Connections from the sympathetic chain run via the hypogastric plexus to the large colon, kidney, urinary bladder, and sex organs.

The parasympathetic division of the autonomic nervous system also originates mostly from the intermediolateral cell column of the spinal cord. The parasympathetic supply to the head is carried by the third, seventh, and ninth cranial nerves. The tenth cranial nerve (vagus), which runs via the cardiac and pulmonary plexuses, supplies the heart and lungs. The vagus supply also connects with the esophageal plexus, then runs to the celiac plexus, where it supplies the stomach, liver, pancreas, and spleen. A part of the vagal supply then runs adjacent to the aorta and sends a branch to the small intestine. Another vagal branch travels to the hypogastric plexus, thence to the large intestine; another branch of the vagus supplies the kidney and urinary bladder, while the last vagal branch supplies the sex organs.

The above is merely an anatomical outline of these two main branches which make up the autonomic nervous system, so that most bodily organs and structures contain both parasympathetic and sympathetic nerve supplies. However, the sympathetic portion of the autonomic system, according to Milner (2), is particularly involved with emotional stress, since its influence is more widespread than that exerted by the parasympathetic division.

The two portions of the autonomic nervous system act opposite to one another, since the sympathetic portion makes the heart beat increase while the parasympathetic component slows it down. This action of these two autonomic components is termed reciprocal inhibition (3), according to Krech et al.

In a previous chapter we discussed the hypothalamus. Krech terms it the "head ganglion" of the autonomic nervous system, and rightfully so, because injuries to it produce all sorts of injury to metabolic, temperature, and organ structures. Our immunologic theory teaches that the hypothalamus and other cortical and subcortical centers become hypersensitized to excessive psychoimmunogens. It will be well to remember this important point as we examine some chemical changes which are produced by neural stimuli in the autonomic nervous system.

Chemistry of the Autonomic Nervous System

The chemistry of the autonomic nervous system has been recently advanced markedly by many outstanding physiologists; not the least of these brilliant investigators was Sir Henry Dale of England. It has been shown that the parasympathetic portion of the autonomic nervous system possesses a cholinergic action on the reacting cells of a hollow organ, such as the stomach. This system produces acetylcholine adjacent to the location where such a nerve enters the organ wall.

On the sympathetic nerve supply side, neural stimulation forms acetylcholine, which is produced between the first and second neurones that carry the neural stimulus to the reacting cells where sympathin is formed. This is an epinephine (adrenalin)-like material with an opposite reaction to that of acetylcholine. Epinephrine causes the blood vessels, that supply skeletal muscles to become dilated and also produces vasoconstriction of the splanchnic viscera. Norepinephrine causes vasoconstriction. Cholinesterase in nerve endings changes acetylcholine to acetic acid and choline (4). This entire subject is quite complicated, and it should be studied further from a physiological textbook.

Psychosomatics (Psychophysiological Diseases)

This term *psychophysiological diseases* has superseded the older term *psychosomatic diseases*. Every now and then someone substitutes a new for an older term. The diseases do not change in nature.

When I attended medical school, I kept a list of all psychologic implications which seemed to be involved with the various diseases. This was continued during my internship, so that my notebooks of that day contained several hundred references. None of the medical textbooks of that day contained such information, and I harbored the idea that some day I would launch a journal on this matter.

At that time, Professor Helen Flanders Dunbar, of New York City, began writing about similar data. I corresponded with her, and she invited me to meet with her in New York. So I brought the data I had collected during the years with me. However, this being my first visit to that big city, I heard about New York's famous Chinatown and the marvelous food they prepared. It so happened that my meeting with Professor Dunbar became delayed for four hours as I enjoyed superb Chinese cuisine. When I finally did meet with Professor Dunbar, she was understandably upset by the delay I had caused, and I apologized. But after a few cocktails, we agreed that psychosomatic medicine, as she termed it, deserved a definite place in the medical field. I gave her my data and returned home. Not too long thereafter, H. Flanders Dunbar, M.D., Ph. D., as she preferred to be called, had her famous volume published on psychosomatic medicine. This was the start for this entirely new contribution of psychiatry to medicine. Now there are sections of psychophysiological medicine, with their own professors, which have become an important part of many departments of psychiatry in our medical schools.

Psychophysiological problems can be said to have been caused by hyperactive autonomic systems; these troubles, I believe, originate because of hypersensitizations of the learning centers in the cerebral cortex, which Clark Hull termed overlearning. These centers, via the Leyden Jar Principle, produce excessive neural stimuli which travel back and forth through the Papez-MacLean circuitry to and from the subcortical centers which, in turn become hypersensitized to the excessive neural stimuli. Added neural impulses from the hypersensitized cerebral cortex and the subcortical centers finally spill into the autonomic nervous system (sympathetic and parasympathetic systems), thence into what we term the target visceral organs, which, in turn, become overstimulated or hypersensitized. This huge chain of events finally produce the psychophysiologic disorders.

Some individuals seem more prone to develop certain hypersensitizations of a particular organ, while others become susceptible to overstimulations of other organs. It is not known at this time exactly what factors determine the particular organ that becomes involved in these hypersensitization processes. Possibly some inherited weakness is controlling.

Psychologists and psychiatrists place the blame on the production of anxiety, but this is merely a symptom which results from repeated frustratory events that are perceived in the subcortical structures. It is highly important to remember that multiple frustrations, or even one major frustration, can produce pain. As will be repeated often in this volume, painful situations (as Darwin emphasized) cause the affected pain-racked individual either to fight the source of the pain or to run from it.

Prolonged states of anxiety can produce structural changes in the subcortical organs. These can hypertrophy (enlarge) and produce excessive stimulations of the autonomic nervous system that affect the organs they supply with excessive neural stimulations. Thus, many glands, vascular structures, and smooth muscles become affected, as do various hormonal and metabolic functions. Hence, we can note that emotional upheavals are intimately connected with many physiologic processes that can produce aggression, hostility, feelings of guilt, and various forms of anxiety and depression in humans and in some of the higher animals, as described so clearly by Akiskal and McKinney (5). One's ability or inability to handle stress often may be the determining factor as to whether or not he may develop a psychophysiologic disorder. Noyes and Kolb (6) have published a comprehensive list of the various psychophysiological disorders which can involve the circulatory, gastrointestinal, musculoskeletal, respiratory, endocrine, skin, genitourinary, and nervous systems.

Few people are alone in this world. Usually they are surrounded by others, which brings us to considerations that involve the subject of social psychology. Dorfman (7) stressed its importance as to the genesis of psychophysiological disorders when he stated that Darwin's fight or flight concept at times becomes thwarted by society's imposed standards of civilization and its so-called ethics. Thus, fear, rage and other emotions may become suppressed for a time, but these tend to emerge in types of behavior induced through the autonomic system. These can arise from autogenous or heterogenous sources (8).

Allow me to stress a highly novel and important concept at this point. It concerns the difference between neural stimulations and neural sensitizations. If I become aware of the approach of a roaring, speeding car through my auditory and visual senses, I might remark on this speeding car and its inherent dangers. But if the car's occupants fire a shotgun in the air or at me, my reactions might become intensified markedly. I might react by falling to the ground or by shaking my fist. The first episode involved my reactions through hearing and seeing the car, while my responses to the second episode became markedly accentuated because of the shotgun blast. The first scene produced reactions through neural stimuli, while the second event produced sensitizing reactions which were of much greater intensity. Yet, both episodes involved identical neural stimuli and their tracts, but with different stimuli intensities. Another major difference was that the first even probably would have been of short duration so far as my memory is concerned. But the last episode would be far longer lasting. I might remember that event for a long time, and I might attempt to find the individuals who fired the shotgun in my direction. Furthermore, the first event probably would have raised my blood pressure for a short time, if at all. But the sensitizing effects from the second scene might have caused glycosuria to have been found in my urine sample. I might never have forgotten such a terrifying experience as was presented by the second episode.

It seems rather obvious that we are dealing with the nature, the size of the dosage, the length of time such afferent stimuli operated, and whether or not a similar experience had been previously recorded or encoded within my cerebral archives. In other words, the amount and the nature of stimuli seems all-important for both episodes. Excessive stimuli therefore appear not alone to be able to stimulate the organism to action, but to possess the important property of sensitizing and even hypersensitizing the target areas of perception (cerebral cells) in an individual. This seems to be a very important basic point which has not received enough interest until now. As with other immunologic reactions, the size (dosage) of the immunogen or the psychoimmunogen appears to determine the degree of the response in any normal individual. It is essentially the body's reaction to injury, if such stimuli happen to be excessive and tend to produce pain.

The Psyche-Soma Concept

This psyche-soma (mind-body) concept is an unfortunate dichotomy. The brain's physiology is dependent directly upon its functioning parts. Its anatomy should not become severed from the rest of the body's anatomy and physiology. All are integral parts which are dependent upon one another, since its behavioral direction arises from the brain and its component parts. This mind-body concept is as nebulous as are faith, hope, and charity along with "meaningful dialogue" and the blatant and continual use of "y'know" with one's speech. The following old saw is similarly appropos: What happens to one's lap when he stands up?

The Genesis of a Psychosomatic Diarrheal Reaction

Kindly allow me to digress a bit to explain this reaction more fully. During my early childhood, we had a barn on our home lot. This structure formerly housed dad's horse, called King. He was a shiny black stallion that seemed to delight in racing and passing every other horse he saw, much to the consternation of my mother, who was taken many times on wild dashes down the streets. But King brought my dad and his surgical packs in short order to many a farmhouse where a badly diseased appendix was removed as the patient lay on the kitchen table.

But King finally gave way to progress and a 1910 Cadillac, which was equipped with shiny brass headlights and windshield braces. The barn then became a clubhouse for our gang. The old harnesses and the horsy odors of that place still remain in my cerebral archives! One noon I shoved open the loft door of the barn. I became aware of a perfect parabola from the urinary stream as I voided from this second story loft. Just then up the driveway appeared my father with another doctor from a nearby community as they parked the Cadillac. They must have observed also this demonstration of Newton's law of gravity, but they never mentioned it to me.

Now we approach the crux of the matter. One day I took the lunch pail to the father of one of our gang. He worked in a local paper mill. But as I returned homeward, I saw billows of smoke and heard the clatter of galloping horses' hoofs accompanied by the clanging gongs of the fire department. I ran in that direction and met another boy who yelled to me that our barn was on fire! Sure enough, when I arrived at the fiery scene, there was my boyhood idol, Chief McGillan, who was shouting orders from the hook and ladder rig as the three snorting and sweaty horses were detached from the firewagon. A giant boiler with a short smoke stack characterized the steamer wagon. It belched sparks surrounded by dense blackish grey clouds of smoke. Water pressure was increased by the pumping movements from the pistons as they spit out steam which caused the flywheel to spin crazily. Three hose streams of water from this equipment played upon the burning barn. These fire fighters were real heroes!

After the barn had been doused adequately with water, my dad and Chief McGillan led me to our living room where I was questioned as to who started the blaze. I didn't know, and I still don't to this day.

After the hubbub subsided we had our noon meal. I shall never forget the main dish was chipped beef in a cream sauce on toast. I soon grew ill with severe abdominal cramps, and I left the table and ran upstairs to the bathroom where I had a severe diarrheal reaction. Even years later, the mention of chipped beef in cream sauce would shortly lead to severe abdominal cramps and diarrhea! Here was my first introduction to a psychosomatic manifestation! This example can be reduced to the following formula:

1. Seeing the burning barn ⎱ ⎰ abdominal cramps
2. Seeing the dish of chipped beef⎰ ⎱followed by diarrhea

In a way, these behavioral reactions have the earmarks of a conditioned response. But this differs from such a reaction because of (1) its intensity, and (2) its longevity, which are the characteristics of a sensitizing reaction. The mechanisms for the production of both types of reactions are quite similar, to be sure, and appear to be dependent upon sensitizing doses of psychoimmunogens which have been intense in amounts and which finally produce hypersensitivity.

Limbic System and Psychosomatics

As Doty (9) stresses so aptly, the external world's stimuli play upon the neocortex, while emotion and affect are spawned by the limbic system, which also regulates endocrine and autonomic reactions of the individual. These can be exemplified by the fight-or-flight pattern and other motivational behavior such as seeking nourishment, temperature control, sexual behavior, maternal responses, etc. All are associated intimately with the individual's basic needs. Disorders of the limbic system produce psychosomatic difficulties through their autonomic outlets to the target organs or structures from the subcortical organs.

Exteroceptive (perceptual) stimuli are responsible for learning. Without the ability to perceive harmful stimuli which originate from one's environment, the individual so affected cannot respond adequately to such stimuli, and death may ensue at a very early date. Given the all-important ability to stimulate, or better still, to *sensitize* the individual and therefore make him aware of danger from toxic and excessive environmental stimuli, an early and necessary form of learning takes place. It results in cortical cell encoding which produces changes in these receptor cortical cells of a neuroelectrochemical nature. These changes are stored (library theory) and are recalled (memory response) at will through one's volition or, better still, through association of ideas. These cortical changes follow exteroceptive stimuli and are the main types of cerebration.

Interoceptive stimuli, generated in the neocortex, travel via the Papez-MacLean pathways to the limbic cortex, which is believed to produce emotional and affective feelings. It is not known as yet how the neocortex can generate such interoceptive stimuli as being able to sensitize or even to hypersensitize the neocortical receptive cells rather than merely stimulate them, perhaps we might have a lead as to how such resultant interoceptive neural discharges of potentials may ensue. This is based on the author's use of a Leyden jar-like discharge that may result from hypersensitized states in overly sensitized cortical cells, and this process may be similar to the cortical discharges that produce dreams. The resultant surmenage of neural potentials then travel through the Papez-MacLean circuitry to and from the limbic system (10).

Here, again, the question posed previously reasserts itself. Is it merely neural stimulation which affects these limbic nuclei, or could this be basically a sensitizing process? If the latter, an entirely new approach to limbic physiology is indicated, with various possibilities that would not be present merely with stimulation from neural impulses of interoceptive origin. The concept of neural sensitizations to those target organs which can produce psychosomatic effects is important, because hypersensitizing these organs the bronchial tree, the gut, vascular tree, etc.—might introduce a wide span of immunologic results. Studies to substantiate this concept might well produce a plethora of advances in our knowledge of psychosomatic pathophysiology and its therapy. Why one target area thus succumbs to psychosomatic pathophysiology while another area escapes might be explained through immunologic mechanisms. To my knowledge, such an approach has not been undertaken.

Limbic System and Psychoses

Some investigators believe the Limbic system may be involved intimately with the psychoses. As an example, certain neurochemical changes have been discovered recently in schizophrenia and in psychoses. Among these abnormal findings, the sweat of such patients was discovered to contain an abnormal aliphatic material termed trans-2 methyl-2 hexenoic acid that was not found in the sweat of normal individuals (11). Added to this highly interesting observation, Noval and Mao (12) found an unidentified antigen to be present in an abnormal amount in the serum from schizophrenic patients with the use of an immunodiffusion procedure. This unidentified antigen may later be shown to be composed of two or more antigens. Here again, the decided value from employing immunologic investigative procedures for studying schizophrenic pathophysiology has been demonstrated.

So the limbic system appears involved with certain behavioral abnormalities as exemplified by some psychoses, and probably also with the formation of psychosomatic disorders. Perhaps the fundamental cause or causes may be related to hypersensitization of the limbic apparati by excessive interoceptive stimuli that originate from the neocortical centers. Thus, hypersensitization of the receptor organs involved with structures that innervate these tissues may occur. Repeated excessive interoceptive stimuli may be responsible for the overt behavioral abnormalities that are observed with the various forms of psychosomatic pathophysiology. We return to our basic concept that neural afferent stimuli, wherever these occur, not alone stimulate but also can sensitize or even hypersensitize their receptive end organs. As previously mentioned (13) these neural transfers of electrical potential appear to depend upon the size, nature, the length of time these stimuli operate, and upon whether or not previous similar neural stimuli have affected these recipient neural centers in the neocortex or even the limbic system.

Recent investigations involving lesion and stimulation of the basal ganglia seem to show the role the globus pallidus plays in the organization and direction of primates for goal oriented behavior. Travis and Sparks (14) of the University of Alabama's Department of Psychology have uncovered some highly significant observations about these basal ganglia in which the phenomena of attention and set are implicated.

Environmental stress responses mainly concern the sympathetic nervous system (15), while the peripheral autonomic ganglia, with the hypophysis and brain stem, are concerned with blood pressure and respiratory changes. Digestion and excretion mainly involve the parasympathetic system. In summary, the autonomic nervous system is intimately concerned with the individual's survival, and the hypothalamus serves as a direct link between endocrine physiology and the individual's central nervous system.

Stimulation vs. Sensitization

The stimulation of the autonomic nervous system produces behavioral reactions to one's environment. But this behavior results from bodily response to environmental changes, which may involve neural stimulations *plus* sensitizing reactions because of such repeated stimuli. Then the ensuing hypersensitization of these involved visceral structures becomes apparent. Such sensitizing or hypersensitizing reactions of these affected organs might explain how they become directly involved with psychosomatic disorders. As with the learning reactions in cortical cells, the degree of psychosomatic pathophysiologic changes might be dependent upon the nature, size (caliber), and duration of such visceral (autonomic) stimuli, plus whether or not previously associated stimuli have affected such target areas. Here, then, is a *modus operandi* for the pathogenesis of psychosomatic diseases. The real importance of the visceral brain or limbic systems now emerges (16).

Investigators employing operant conditioning techniques in the U.S.S.R. and this country have demonstrated that heart rates, blood pressure readings, and even hepatic cells may respond to such controlled operant stimuli. Employing such operant (instrumental) procedures, the possibility appears that even psychosomatic disorders might be eventually treated by these same methods. Coupled with the concept that these diseases might be studied and controlled in accordance with immunologic principles such as we have outlined, improved therapy may well result.

9

Frustration

Frustration can cause pain which might produce depression. Frustration does not produce a pleasurable sensation, so that few if any individuals will laugh or feel gleeful as a result of it. Frustration has produced many tears as most people will relate. People who are hungry become frustrated. The alcoholic individual and the habitual user of drugs become frustrated when their various supplies are cut off. Frustration can produce hostility. Ask the United Nations about this, for repeated frustrations to a nation can produce a war when enough people become involved deeply, expecially with repeated socioeconomic frustrations. So frustrations can affect an individual, a family, a large group of people, a nation, or even groups of nations.

Frustrations can occur because of slight or serious emotional upheavals. A person can become frustrated when his wife serves him a cold cup of coffee, or he could suffer a major frustration if he were to play for the world chess championship and $100,000 on the winner-take-all basis. If he were to lose the match, not alone would he become frustrated; he might well suffer a deep depression as the result of his defeat. All frustrations can become painful. The sites for these unhappy reactions are in the subcortical areas which spawn the emotions. No frustrations are present when a person becomes elated by overwhelming success, since elation is the opposite to the depression that can be produced by frustration. To use the Freudian term, no ambivalence exists in such a case. The worker who, for one reason or another, is not paid becomes frustrated and a bit angry. The person who adds a column of figures incorrectly repeatedly also becomes frustrated and angry. The inability of a particular beautiful woman to win a beauty contest must be frustrating to her, to say the least. She might even attempt to smile through her tears. Should she happen to win the contest, her tears are for happiness and result from overstimulation of her autonomic nervous system. She is definitely not depressed, not, at least, for the time being!

Every psychologic event is predicated upon previous learning. If this were not true, then the individual would have the mentality of a block of wood, for even the lowly paramecia react to their environment and learn thereby.

If an individual becomes frustrated enough and possesses a normal degree of intelligence, we can foresee he is bound to learn something from his frustration. He will, in the future at least, attempt to remedy or avoid the source or sources which have produced his frustrations. Frustrations in an individual can spill over to others who may be faced with similar painful situations.

The entire subject of learning is so important, it appears to me at least, that I believe the student's first course in psychology should be devoted to the entire subject of learning with its many ramifications. This would afford adequate preparation so he could more easily comprehend further psychologic studies. The same approach could be adapted also for students of psychiatry.

So learning with its resultant frustrations can play a very important role in generating adverse behavior such as hostility or depressions in animals and humans (1). These types of behavior in humans have played particularly significant roles in triggering public protestations, demonstrations, and civil disobedience. A great deal has been written and spoken on frustratory reactions in humans, but to my knowledge, no one has made an attempt to classify them.

Ethics and the laws made by one's society are weakened or forcibly replaced, temporarily at least, by the aggressions of the stronger over weaker members as the result of constant competition over many physical, physiologic, and psychologic matters of social importance. Here the masses assume the offensive rather than the individual. History is rife with persons who assumed leadership during public struggles for power. One can easily recall such men as Napoleon, the Caesars, Hitler, and Castro, who stand out as exploiters of such politicoeconomic struggles.

Should these leaders and their followers become defeated, for one reason or another, these individuals withdraw, escape if possible from their frustratory environments, and may easily suffer depressions that can well lead to suicide. Hitler's example will suffice for the moment.

Obviously, constant competition occurs throughout one's life span, and it can begin at a very early age. Competition, often resulting in frustration, continues constantly in almost every human endeavor, and it is extremely noticeable in the business world where individuals and their organizations vie for supremacy of political power and economic gain almost constantly. Pick up any newspaper and read the ads where one group will attempt to outbid the other in this never ending competition for financial gain.

Some individuals, groups, and business chains will not be able to compete well enough to win such political and economic battles. The resulting defeats can produce frustrations that are expressed quite frequently by hostility towards the tormentor or tormentors. As I write this, I think of the Watergate incident and its seemingly never-ending ramifications. But such social reactions certainly are not limited to humans. They are observed quite readily throughout the entire animal kingdom. So the behavior of the individual is intertwined with social psychology or, in other words, with the behavior of others.

Puppies seize food from their weaker litter mates, and the tough little human kid grabs toys from his weaker brother. The business tycoon forecloses on his competitor (never on

Sunday) or undersells him, driving him to possible bank-
ruptcy or some other type of ruin, which often takes the form
of depression and possible suicide. This is the game of life,
if one can call it that unblushingly. This offensive behavior
exemplifies a Spencerian version of the Darwinian concept
that only the fittest survive.

The adherence to numerous and varied religious teachings
has not diminished nor have these appeared to control adequately the many unethical practices that are present constantly evident in democratic, communist, and monarchist
societies. Such unethical practices can become especially
rampant and virulent wherever anarchy exists.

Frustration has been employed as a catchall term. Silver
(2) stressed the frustrations experienced when considering
the reading problem of dyslexia. He mentioned the frustrations to be overcome in dealing with complex reading
problems. He mentioned the frustrations produced by the
gap in knowledge, the frustrations of teachers and school ad-
ministrators, the frustrations of researchers and practition-
ers, and the frustrations of parents who wish to help their
children with various reading disabilities.

Frustration, a most interesting psychologic phenomenon,
is defined as "a condition of increased emotional tension resulting from failure to achieve sought gratifications and satisfaction ordinarily as a result of forces outside of one's self"
(3). Another definition, and perhaps a better one, is "the
condition that results when an impulse to act or the completion of an act is blocked out or thwarted, preventing the
satisfaction of attainment" (4).

Deese and Hulse (5) stressed that organisms can be frustrated experimentally in various ways. Wolman (6) observed that, in some humans, frustration is accepted with
little change, while in others even a mild frustration produces unbearable consequences. Hofling (7) writes that
frustration can lead to hostility, which he thinks is both inevitable and automatic in infants, and I might add, is also

often evident in adults of all ages and both sexes.

The term *frustration* is employed psychologically and psychiatrically in one huge, neat, and undifferentiated package. We shall dissect and examine frustration further under magnification to determine, if possible, its basic structures and the mechanisms that can produce its emotional upheavals.

Some energy or force is necessary to cause frustration. This energy which interferes with or prevents the attainment of the individual's goal is termed the *frustrator*. The organism or any part of it becoming inhibited or inactivated by a frustrator is termed the *frustrant*. In common parlance, we must know who (frustrator) is doing what to whom (frustrant).

Frustration can occur only in a viable organism or animal, invertebrate or vertebrate. The harmful effects, which include pain and injury, may be either temporary or permanent, partial or complete by its interference with one or more physiologic or psychologic funtions in the viable frustrant who also must be aware (conscious) of such events.

Frustration can affect the individual through his own actions, as exemplified by the young person with acne who insists upon rupturing pustules on his face and digging out comedones (blackheads), thereby causing scarring of the skin. The pain from severe frustrations might become unbearable, and then one might attempt suicide. Such reactions to frustration are called *auto-frustration*, since the individual himself becomes the frustrator. Or frustration can be caused by outside forces, as exemplified by murder or even death from acts of God, as by the production of injuries or even death from lightning, tornadoes, hurricanes, or earthquakes. These are called *heterofrustrants*. The culminating frustrant produces death itself, either from an auto-frustrator or from a heterofrustrator. Freud might have enjoyed a field day, had he considered these possibilities.

Hebb (8) mentions that problem-solving involves certain elements of frustration which can contribute to sources of pleasure as with the playing of chess or bridge. In such situations, should the stakes be minor, the frustration is usually of minor import and can be temporary in its effect. But with the primary dyslexic person (9), the frustrant is probably congenital in type and permanent because of the inability of Broadman's cerebral areas 18 and 19 to assimilate and interpret properly the neuroelectrochemical changes which normally occur during the learning (encoding of the brain), storage, and recall of data arising from frustration.

The various sites of action, whereby frustrators can act upon frustrants, should be presented. This may assist in the further comprehension of inhibiting reactions resulting from frustrations.

Frustrators can involve any portion of the sensory (perceptive) system; these are afferent in type and can be exemplified by the application of an eye patch over the frustrant's eye. This blocks vision for that involved eye. Any sensory receptor and its nerve tracts to the brain can be involved by a frustrator. Thus, impacted cerumen (wax) affects audition in an involved ear. Certain tumors or disease processes can disrupt the perceptual avenues of sensoria; also other similar frustrators can cause disabilities within the other afferent systems. Such frustrations are peripheral in nature.

When frustrators involve the cerebrum, cerebellum, the subcortical centers, and the medulla with their various interconnecting neural pathways, the *cortical* or *central* types of frustration occurs. Examples are numerous, but a few will suffice, such as the effects from anaesthetics, tumors, various disease processes, traumas to these areas, hypnotic trances, and various psychotropic drug effects which can involve anatomical areas of the brain.

The motor pathways (efferent neural tracts) which leave the brain can become frustrated by similar pathologic events. Some examples are the frustrations produced by body, arm, or leg casts, poliomyelitis, and other disease entities. The use of handcuffs or straightjackets and related frustrators interfere mainly with one's muscular activities. A leg amputation is a severe permanent example of this type of frustration.

Similarly, the autonomic nervous system can be affected by various frustrators as by sympathectomies, the neoplasms, and traumas that interfere with various aspects of autonomic physiology, such as flushing, blushing, and sweating. Also the genesis of various psychophysiologic (psychomatic) disorder of the autonomic system is produced by repeated frustrations that finally cause a conflict between the parasympathetic and the sympathetic autonomic nerve components to the skin.

Marshall-White Syndrome (10, (11), (12)

This disorder can be observed readily in individuals of both sexes and in all races. It manifests itself through the observation of small whitish spots, up to about eight millimeters in width, which are imposed on a reddish skin background on the palms of the hands, lower legs, and feet, and very rarely on the skin of the chest. These whitish areas of vasoconstriction very slowly change their forms, for some of these whitish skin patches may coalesce with other patches. These involved skin areas are four tenths of a degree cooler than their surrounding areas, when measured with a thermocouple.

Usually associated with this disorder of the autonomic nervous system is the presence of insomnia, sinus arrhythmia, and a tendency for the victim to be the "fall guy" who has been subjected to multiple frustrations and has run rather than fought for his rights. He is the retiring type of person.

This syndrome with its vasoconstrictive white, mascular patches can be observed in such patients if his hands are allowed to remain lowered at his side for a few minutes.

Placing the hands of such an involved individual under ultra-violet light enables these vasoconstricted patches to be observed very readily.

This skin disorder is caused by repeated frustrations that have produced pain affecting the subcortical brain areas and thence the autonomic nervous system. A conflict becomes evident in the involved skin areas, readily noted in the palmar surfaces. Skin blanching is produced, caused by vaso-constriction that slowly gives way to vasodilation of the microcirculation.

Many of my students have observed such changes in others, and they have been readily able to diagnose severe previous frustrations in people who show this syndrome. Such people tend to be of a nervous disposition; they dislike violence, and they appear to be overly sensitive to their eco-systems, which have hypersensitized them because of their many previous painful episodes. These individuals are, for the most part, kindly, highly sensitive persons who, as the saying has it, wouldn't hurt a flea.

10

Anatomical

Orientation

The anatomy of the human skull, the brain, and its contents is intricate. A great deal of study is needed to understand their many parts. It is not intended to describe them in detail herein. The reader is urged to become acquainted with their anatomy and physiology from such sources, as college courses and textbooks.

A mechanic is at a loss to understand why a car motor is malfunctioning unless he is well acquainted with its separate parts and their functions. Similarly, the psychologist cannot expect to understand how the brain is made, how and why it functions, until he has mastered most of its many anatomic and physiologic intricacies.

Evans (1) called attention to the human skull as being constructed similarly to a square box. This box, the skull, protectively encloses the brain. At the base of this box is a rather large opening, the foramen magnum, from which the spinal cord emerges. Inside this box and covering the brain substance are three separate tissues. I help my students remember the tissue names through the initials "D" "A" "P." Beginning from the skull there is the dura, a rather heavy, tough membrane. The next tissue is a weblike covering, the arachnoid, which resembles the spider's web from whence it received its name. Directly over the brain itself is the pia matter. So, as Evans emphasized so aptly, the skull is virtually a closed box which covers and protects the delicate brain substance.

One is reminded readily as to the inadequacy of the skull's ability to protect the brain, particularly during the present age of motorcycles, high-rise construction, football, ice hockey, and polo, where the chances for brain injuries are particularly high and rampant. So these participants in such dangerous endeavors wear various forms of protective plastic caps to further protect their skulls and brains from possible injuries. Laws have been passed to enforce the wearing of such protective devices.

The largest portions of the brain are the two cerebral hemispheres. These have attained their highest development in the human. Under the cerebral cortex, contained in the hemispheres, are the basal ganglia, the thalamus and the hypothalamus. But superior to (above) these two latter structures is the corpus collosum, an arched white structure. The front (anterior) portion is termed the genu (knee), and the back (posterior) covers the midbrain. It is through the corpus collosum that the two cerebral hemispheres are connected by various neural pathways which run to and from each cerebral hemisphere.

Each hemisphere contains a frontal, parietal, temporal, and occipital lobe. The neo-cortex contains six layers of fibers which are associated with sensory and motor projections found in the cerebral hemispheres. The motor portion is located in the frontal lobe, the parietal lobe is associated with sensory intake. The temporal lobe receives auditory stimuli, while the occipital lobe contains visual receptors.

The limbic system or visceral brain (2), mentioned by Chusid and McDonald, is highly important to psychologists, since this structure is connected with recent loss of memory (hippocampus), motivation, rage and fear, and sexual behavior. These also involve the rhinencephalon, containing the hypothalamus, amygdala, septal nuclei, the anterior thalamic nuclei, and the infolded hippocampus. The limbic system communicates with the medial forebrain and carries afferent and efferent neural fibers, according to MacLean (3).

The basal ganglia are of great importance to psychologists and psychiatrists. They are the life-supporting areas and produce various emotions. They are situated deep in the cerebral hemispheres. As mentioned before, the corpus striatum connects the two cerebral hemispheres, and it contains the internal capsule whose whitish fascicles are found between the caudate nuclei and the gray putamen. The caudate nucleus is located near the lower part of the anterior horn of the lateral ventricle. The posterior limb of the internal capsule separates the thalamus from the caudate nucleous and the lentiform nucleus, composed of the putamen and the globus pallidus. The amygdaloid nucleus lies below the caudate nucleus.

These anatomic structures are intricate, and it would serve the student well to study these and other neurologic structures in the various anatomical textbooks in order to obtain an adequate understanding of their relationships to each other.

The diencephalon covers the third ventricle of the brain. The diencephalon includes the geniculate bodies, the subthalamus, the hypothalamus, and the epithalamus in the thalamic body or structure, which is mainly concerned with sensory perception.

The mid-brain contains many important structures as does the brain stem, including the pons, the medulla, and the cerebellum. Many more important points should be mastered, such as spinal fluid circulation, the brain's intricate blood supply, and other important related subjects, which this limited volume cannot present because the brain's anatomy is highly intricate and difficult to master.

Cranial Nerves

Of the twelve cranial nerves, only those nerves connected with sensory perception are important to us at this time. The first cranial nerve is the olfactory nerve. It is really a fibre tract from the brain. The olfactory nerve originates in the nasal mucosa via ciliated receptors which go through the cribiform part of the ethmoid bone to the olfactory bulb and thence to the hippocampal and the subcollosal gyri where the olfactory stria go to the hippocampus and to the pyriform area and thence via the fornix to the mamillary bodies and the anterior thalamic nuclei.

One of the most important cranial nerves, for our consideration, is the second cranial nerve—the optic nerve, also a fibre tract of the brain which is concerned with sight. The rods and cones of the retina run into the myelinated fibers of the optic nerve and pass to the optic chiasma. Here the nasal half of the optic nerve fibers cross over, while the temporal half remain uncrossed. (This is the way a two-horse team was hitched in order to drive them properly.) The isolated halves of the optic nerves run into the optic tract to the lateral geniculate bodies and superior colliculi where these pass to the calcarine occiptal cortex of the brain.

The acoustic is the eighth cranial nerve, and it is concerned with hearing. It, too, is very important for our consideration. The eighth nerve really consists of two separate portions; the vestibular branch is concerned with man's position in space (proprioceptives), while the cochlear branch is connected with hearing. This is one of the important ways the individual becomes cognizant of his environment. Therefore, stress shall be given to it for our purposes. The tiny ear bones—the incus, malleus, and stapes—set up neural impulses to the organ of Corti to the trapezoid body and lateral lemnisci to the medial geniculate bodies, thence, via the auditory radiations, to the auditory cortex, and they become also associated with the eye muscle nuclei.

The sense of taste, also of importance to the processes of learning, is composed of three separate cranial nerves, the fifth cranial nerve (trigeminal), the facial or seventh cranial nerve, and the ninth or glossopharyngeal nerve, all of which contribute to the tongue's ability to differentiate between sweet, bitter, and salty sensations. The ninth cranial nerve supplies the back (posterior) portions of the tongue, while the fifth and seventh cranial nerves supply the front (anterior) two-thirds of the tongue, where most taste stimuli arise. The tracts to the brain are very involved and are of main interest to students of neurology rather than for our present purposes.

Pain, Touch, and Temperature Tracts

These nerve tracts are of special importance to the learning processes, because the Montessori system is built mainly on the individual's touch perception, which depends upon the exteroceptors. These are specialized cells found in the skin (integument) and they are important in picking up environmental changes. For touch and hair cells, Merkel's and Meissner's corpuscles are involved. Cold is noted through Krause's end bulbs, while warmth is registered by Ruffini's cylinders. Free nerve endings pick up painful stimuli. All these are connected with spinal root ganglia and thence with homologous cranial nerve ganglia that run via the brain stem to the post central gyrus of the cerebral cortex. The various spinal tracts that bring stimuli to the brain should be studied carefully by the student.

11

Immunologic Psychology
in Action:
Cases of
Hypersensitization

When students are asked why they take my courses, invariably they reply that they want to know why people act as they do. In other words, they wish to understand the mechanisms of behavior.

According to Sir Isaac Newton: (1) Every object will continue in motion or rest in a straight line unless some force changes it, (2) the force which causes such change in motion is equal to the acceleration of the object and the product of its mass, (3) the interacting of particles produce the force which acts on one object from another and is equal and opposite to the original force. Newton's Laws of Motion are observable when one billiard ball hits another that happens to be at rest, when we seem to be pushed backwards as we sit in a car that happens to accelerate suddenly, or when we are pitched forward when the car's brakes are suddenly engaged.

Can my reader correlate the Newtonian laws of motion with points I have stressed regarding frustration? Frustration, as you will recall, arises from the inability of an individual to attain a goal. What keeps him from this? Didn't this result because some force, whether external or internal, interferes with the individual's afferent, cortical, or efferent nerve tracts and his previous learning? Such interference occurs every second of the day. It is a marvel, and a testimony of man's flexibility, that coutless more people are not critically frustrated by the negative forces (pressures, applications of energy) abounding in our total environment.

When the frustrated person is finally forced to either fight or run for survival, trouble begins. The affected individual becomes hostile or seeks escape (temporarily at least) from his painful reality through asocial behavior, such as excessive gambling, use of drugs, undesirable sexual activities of various sorts, or other well known escape mechanisms, characterized by anxiety reactions, depressions, or both. He may become psychotic, and reality may cease to exist for him. At the extreme end of the behavioral spectrum, he becomes a candidate for admission to a mental institution.

We should not forget that ecosystemic stimuli affect each person. The size of dosage, the time element, the physical state of the neural tracts, and whether or not similar afferent forces have already played upon him will determine, in large measure, whether excessive cerebral imprinting (hypersensitization) occurs. Clinical examples of hypersensitizations that produced frustrations, taken from life, will help the reader to understand the ensuing behavioral cycle.

The Security Blanket

Many of my readers must have become attached to their own blankets during their infancy and childhood. Emotional attachment to a blanket or a teddy bear is very common with small children. The object's ability to produce warmth engenders pleasure-producing stimuli that are enhanced by the object's softness and particular texture, its appearance and often its particular smell. Part the child from this particular object of affection and he becomes frustrated; he cries lustily, or he may act in a hostile manner.

Return the loved object, and the child's face turns to smiles. As he matures, social (ecosystemic) pressures finally cause him to abandon his security blanket, which he does with much misgiving, for this object had been a continual source of satisfaction through its pleasure-producing qualities. Now he is forced to seek other pleasure-producing sources, usually emanating from the mother or other dear one. Children love to be held, for pleasure and self reassurance.

While attending the university, I met a famed poet, who was one of my teachers. This brilliant professor had a phobia which kept him confined to his home and the university campus. His emotional disorder had arisen during his childhood from a frightening episode in which he had been scalded by steam from a locomotive. Here was a hypersensitizing reaction, encoded in his cerebral cortex by an excessively painful experience, which had been accentuated by (1) seeing the locomotive emit live steam, (2) hearing the locomotive's hissing as the steam was discharged, (3) smelling the locomotive's smoke, (4) and receiving highly painful tactile stimuli when burned by the jet stream of live steam from the locomotive. He developed an obvious defense reaction from this frustrating and highly painful experience which kept him away from any possible confrontation with another locomotive and the possibility of further injury.

Another example of a hypersensitizing reaction occurred to Mike's wife (see Introduction) who could not live in their home or even city after her husband's death. Too many ecosystemic forces connected with her husband's death had hypersensitized her, so that she had to move elsewhere. Environmental stimuli constantly produced additional painful stimuli.

Another of my patients, a young mother, backed her car down her driveway. She felt a thump as the car ran over something. She immediately stopped the car, got out, and ran back to find her two-year-old daughter sprawled motion-less on the driveway. The upshot of this horrifying experi-ence was that the child spent six weeks in the hospital but made an excellent recovery. In the meantime the mother had developed a very severe psychotic depression and some-time later committed suicide. This unfortunate eventuality began with the mother's hypersensitizations resulting from what she felt and saw as the result of her child's injury.

A brilliant young surgeon was returning home with his wife, who was sitting beside him in the front seat of their car. He did not see or hear the oncoming locomotive as they approached the railroad crossing. His wife was killed im-mediately, but he miraculously escaped unscathed.

From that time on, the doctor avoided that railroad cross-ing by driving many blocks out of his way while leaving and returning home. He did not wish to come in further con-tact with the psychoimmunogens (psychoantigens) which had become associated with the accident and the death of his wife. He soon moved to the west coast further to avoid the scene of his pain-producing and serious frustratory ex-perience.

Such traumatizing situations appear to be stimulus-specific, since each of the above events had its own inherent pain-producing aspects. Such traumatizing encodings of the cerebral cortex are long lasting, and I seriously doubt whether any of these victims will forget their painful experi-ences despite the passage of many years.

The following episode is a fairly well controlled study of human behavior under stress (2). Rather recently, my wife and I were being shown a new university campus by the wife of a faculty member who was driving the car. Suddenly, another driver apparently lost control of his car, which struck two other cars and then headed in our direction. Luckily, he was able to stop his car before it rammed into the rear sec-tion of our car.

Our female friend became visibly pale, nauseated, and narrowly averted shock; she barely was able to park the car in an adjacent filling station driveway. She was unable to talk for some time and bent her body over the steering wheel. Slowly she regained her posture and was able to overcome her near shock. Then she related that she had nearly lost her life in a recent auto collision, and only a few days ago had been in another less serious auto accident. These previous events had hypersensitized our friend.

This case demonstrated the two episodes of serious hypersensitizations her cerebral centers suffered from what she had seen, heard, and felt as results from these accidents. The current strong input of these multiple sensory hypersensitizations ensued when she saw the oncoming car as we sat in her car. These multiple and maximum sensory excitations met recognition within her previously similarly encoded cerebral centers (related to Priestley's Association of Ideas). Then a Leyden jar-like surmenage (rushing outflow) from these seriously hypersensitized and supercharged cortical cells ensued, were transmitted to the motor (efferent) and the autonomic nerve tract outlets, and she reacted as described.

My wife and I were not emotionally disturbed. I doubt whether our systemic blood pressure readings, if taken, would have been elevated. There was no emotional surmenage on our part, because we had not been hypersensitized previously to the psychoimmunogens (psychoantigens) our friend had experienced. She had undergone two episodes marked by the influx and the subsequent encoding of excessive amounts of psychoimmunogens that had hypersensitized her cerebral centers. The additional excessive dose of psychoimmunogens, which occurred as we sat beside her, were sufficient to bring about a severe emotional response. All these episodes were very painful to her and nearly produced syncope (loss of consciousness). She had followed our hallmarks for hypersensitization, including the dosage, the time factor, and the previous hypersensitizing episodes. We did not react similarly because we had not been hypersensitized previously to the specific psychoimmunogens. A male patient consulted this famed psychiatrist because the patient was unable to have coitus unless his sexual partner wore boots. Professor Steckel discovered the reason for his patient's difficulty from an initial experience his patient had had, when his governess seduced him during adolescence. She happened to be wearing boots at that time. He had become hypersensitized to what he saw, heard, and felt during that traumatizing episode. The fact that his governess was wearing boots became an integral part of his cortical hypersensitization processes (Gestalt implication).

I will now cite an example of how other excessive ecosystemic stimuli can affect one's afferent neural tracts. This has to do with energy emanating from ultraviolet light, which can inflict injury upon the unfortunate recipient's visual tracts.

While irradiating a batch of liver extract from some clinical experiments, I failed to wear goggles to protect my eyes from the ultraviolet light rays. About six hours later, I noticed rings which appeared around lights; then later, the presence of grinding pains in my eyes. Soon I became completely blind. I called my wife, who summoned an ophthalmologist who relieved the malady with the use of proper eyedrops.

Should any of my readers doubt that excessive afferent stimuli can produce frustration with its often ensuing hostility, merely phone a friend about every five minutes. Before too long, you will perceive hostility in your friend's voice. Or, continue to interrupt your teacher for some time. Then be prepared for a rapid classroom exit as he demonstrates his hostility towards you.

Multiple frustrations can affect the autonomic nervous system. Attendant physical changes can be observed in the

Marshall-White Syndrome, which is apparently related closely to the disorder known as neurocirculatory asthenia, a disorder discovered by Dr. DaCosta during the Civil War in patients who were upset emotionally. It has many synonyms such as irritable heart, soldier's heart, effort syndrome, and other names. Sighing is a cardinal finding in such patients. Their hearts react to the hyperventilation syndrome. They experience palpitations of the heart, and fatiguability due to anxiety reactions which are related closely to disturbances of one's affect, where the fear of exertion is often present.

Further to explain the Marshall-White Syndrome, one should recall that skin color is dependent upon the amount of unsaturated hemoglobin in the blood (3) contained in the subpapillary veins and the capillaries. So when the hands are dangled, flushing of the skin in these regions tends to occur. The blood vessels in these areas are controlled by peripheral resistance which, in turn, is under control by the sympathetic nervous system through the functioning of vasodilator metabolites, temperature, and even the use of drugs. However, the overactivity of the sympathetic nervous system can produce ischemia (lack of blood with skin blanching) in the skin areas of the hands and feet, as is the case in patients who exhibit the Marshall-White Syndrome. Here there is an autonomic conflict between vasoconstrictor and vasodilator mechanisms in the skin areas, so that one can observe the white patches (macules) amidst the reddened skin areas in such patients. One blanched-out area will slowly give way to reddening, while other white areas tend to enlarge. This is a good sign of autonomic instability resulting from repeated frustrations which, in turn, were caused by anxiety-producing situations in emotionally disturbed individuals. One should remember that the vasomotor centers are connected intimately with the hypothalamus and the reticuloform bodies situated at different levels of the brain stem. So again, the subcortical brain areas, and particularly the hypothalamus, must be considered whenever disorders of affect or emotional imbalance are met. Various neuroleptic drugs affect these centers, probably reducing their hypersensitivities and thereby producing clinical improvement through their therapeutic usages. Some of these newer medications have produced rather amazing results by reducing marked hostility or deep depressions in some patients, so that, a few hours later, they appear more calm and much happier than before the medical therapy.

The impact of prolonged painful incidents, I believe, finally hypersensitizes subcortical centers of the brain involved closely with production of affect and the emotions. In order to escape the further traumatizing situations that so often arise from a hostile and a pain-producing environment, the individual is forced finally to fight or run. This painful environmental wear and tear on the individual tends to produce anxiety, depressive reactions, or both from the hypersensitized hypothalamus and other related structures. Branch, Fowler, and Grant (4) wrote about depressions and anxiety that might well be produced by biologic reactions, which can be really equated further to chemical reactions in the affected structures. These workers have mentioned metabolism, electrolytic balances, the biogenic amines, the adrenocortical hormones, and the action of norepinephrine on the centers of affect and emotions that might well be involved in the genesis of anxiety and depression.

Suicide can be the end result of deeply frustratory and highly painful experiences. In other words, suicide expresses the individual's final and complete frustration—his desire to escape the pain-producing environmental forces that have bombarded his perceptive (afferent) nerves and have hypersensitized the encoding centers of his brain and also its subcortical centers. He cannot retreat further, so he attempts to destroy himself.

12

Pleasure vs.

Pain Producing

Stimuli

Various forms of stimuli (energy gradients) affect the individual from the time he becomes a prenate until he succumbs and passes away. These stimuli originate from one's ecosystem and can prove to be pleasurable or painful, depending upon how the subcortical brain centers interpret the nature of these neural stimuli, based upon the amount or the dosage of these stimuli, their nature, the length of time they operate, and whether or not previous related stimuli have sensitized or hypersensitized the recipient brain centers previously.

The sense of touch is related closely to pain sensation (1). If a dog's back is gently stroked, the canine shows some enjoyment, possibly by wagging his tail or licking our hands. He may show a Pavlovian scratch reflex as his back or belly is rubbed gently. If we were to increase the stimuli of touch by applying additional force to the scratching procedure, the pleasurable sensation in the dog would change abruptly to pain. The dog could well react by growling, snarling, or even attempting to snap at his tormentor.

The phantom limb sensation is both an interesting and a baffling phenomenon. Often when a limb is removed surgically, the patient still perceives painful stimuli so that he believes the removed limb is still present. Gardner (2) writes that these painful sensations which arise from phantom limbs have resulted in even digging up the several parts and straightening out the toes and fingers in order to stop the pain. Gardner mentions that, in folklore, these painful sensations were the work of the devil.

Masochism is another exotic phenomenon connected with painful sensations. In such cases, the patient seeks out painful sensations, typically from brutal beatings by sadistic persons. These two abnormal states appear to be connected closely, particularly when associated with sexual acts. Eaton and Peterson (3) refer to sadomasochistic patients as dominants and submissives, who, I might add, are also to be found among homosexuals.

Concerning actinic rays, as from the sun or a sun lamp, these rays can give pleasurable sensations if received in small or moderate amounts. But excessive amounts of actinic stimuli can cause great pain and may even prove life-threatening.

Sensations produced by motion, as from boating, when gentle swells rock the boat, can be quite pleasurable. But when in choppy seas that rock the boat violently, these sensory stimuli can evoke sea sickness, accompanied by dizziness, nausea, and vomiting, and can make the affected person wish that death would stop the horrible stimuli forever.

Sounds from a symphony orchestra can prove to be highly satisfying, pleasurable, and intriguing. But should members of the orchestra go berserk and the percussion section slam their cymbals, blow their sirens, bang their Chinese gongs, and the like, I am sure the audience would quickly rush for the nearest exits!

Reading in moderate amounts can be highly pleasurable. If done in excess, it can cause the blurring of vision, eyestrain, lacrimation, and even headaches. Nor can a professional wine taster smoke incessantly and remain capable of evaluating the subtle differences in various wines!

It has been amply shown that excessive factory noises

tend to produce deafness. Again, the size of the stimuli (dosage), the length of time these act, the nature of the neural pathways (state of health), and whether or not previous related neural stimuli have acted on the perceptive pathways, all determine how the individual will react.

Manias and Phobias

A few years ago, while reviewing my clinical records, I was impressed with the etiologic differences that existed between manias and phobias. I noted that excessive *painful* incidences contributed to the formation of phobias, while excessive *pleasurable* events appeared to formulate manias (4).

There are many forms of mania. For example, a patient who enjoys outwitting various store personnel by stealing their merchandise is known as a kleptomaniac. A female who obtains her so-called kicks from sexual relations with numerous males, or females, is known as a nymphomaniac. One who derives pleasure from drinking excessive alcoholic beverages is known as a dypsomaniac. A patient who shows morbid exaggeration in sexual behavior or reactions is known as an erotomaniac. The uncontrollable desire to make purchases is called oniomania. All of these forms of abnormal behavior are caused apparently be excessive *pleasurable* impulses which are uncontrollable in individuals so affected.

Phobias appear to be based on *painful* experiences which have produced excessive fear reactions in persons. For example, the morbid fear of sounds or noises is termed phonophobia. Being excessively afraid of water is hydrophobia, which, incidentally, has been appended to the disease known as rabies. Having a dread for snakes is called serpentophobia. The genesis of such a disorder occurred while I was in grade school. While playing in the school yard, another lad removed a garter snake from his pocket. He whirled the serpent by its tail around and around his head.

Finally, the snake's head became severed, and it struck the face of another playmate, who was spattered by the snake's blood. As the result of this painful and highly traumatizing incident, that youngster remained deathly afraid of snakes for the years I knew him. Perhaps he suffers from serpentophobia to this very day.

Token Economy and Reinforcement

In instrumental conditioning, reinforcement is giving a rewarding stimulus to an individual. Or a painful (noxious) stimulus is withdrawn after the subject has affected a proper response (5).

I well recall reading many articles during the '60's which dealt with the so called "token economies" which were being studies in many mental institutions at that ime. Essentially, patients, who had been sitting on the wards for years, were being rewarded with coupons or slips of paper whenever they became motivated to complete a favorable act or task. For example, they received such a token, sometimes in the form of chips that denoted certain values, when they performed worthwhile tasks such as making their beds or sweeping the floor. These tokens could purchase tobacco or give them the opportunity of visiting the city to purchase items of value to the patient. These reinforcements helped to motivate these erstwhile sedentary patients to accomplish tasks they had not been able to accomplish heretofore. The therapeutic gains, observed in such patients, proved to be quite startling in many cases. Other mental hospitals began instituting such procedures with marked success. But whenever a patient refused to work for such a token or reward, he lost a certain number of earned tokens.

Breaking down the above procedures results in the realization that meritorious work, accomplished by these patients, gave rise to the receipt of *pleasurable* stimuli which proved to be strong motivating forces. Whenever the patient regressed and for any reason did not or could not accomplish his goal, he was subjected to the loss of a certain number of his earned tokens. This deprivation proved *painful* to the patient because he was kept from attaining pleasurable sensations by being able to obtain what he desired. In other words, the token economy rewarded (gave pleasurable sensations) the right doer, while he became subjected to painful sensations when his behavior led to wrong doing. Animals and man prefer pleasurable rather than painful stimuli. So this simple situation was applied effectively in the hospital wards.

The basic behavior pattern for such therapeutic applications certainly is not new. Children have been rewarded for good behavior (look what Santa Claus brought you), and they have been punished for adverse behavior (stand in the corner for five minutes). This same procedure is supposedly employed in the business world by platitudes which have preached motivation for centuries. "The early bird gets the worm", "if you don't succeed the first time, try, try again", and many other sayings have attempted to gain the successful motivation of employees, children, students, mental patients, and others.

Pikunas (6) defined reinforcement as a helping influence or situation which increases accepted patterns of behavior. (Cf. conditioning.) Clinical improvement by enhancing pleasurable patient reaction has been attained through the use of occupational and recreational therapies. Attempts are made to bring pleasurable rather than painful stimuli to mental patients, and to reduce their sense of isolation, by allowing them to make decisions when feasible (7).

13

The Ecosystem

and Social

Psychology

The prenate is wholly dependent upon its mother for life itself. But additional environmental stresses act upon it after it becomes free from the mother's womb. What I am attempting to accentuate is that the neonate individual rarely if ever becomes free from ecospheral forces because he or she is really hemmed in by environment. This situation prevails throughout life with the exception of the very few individuals who lead lives like Robinson Crusoe, possibly because of being shot down over enemy lines during wars. However, such a person has environmental forces to contend with.

Consider the varied environmental forces which affect each individual. Mother and father dominate the scene. Then there are sisters and brothers who vie continually for the catbird's seat in the family, not to forget the many relatives of all descriptions, and the peers of the child who come invited or uninvited. Don't forget the many teachers whose job it is to acquaint the learning child with his or her environment. When the child becomes of school age, he is forced into new surroundings which gives rise to zenophobic reactions (hatred of foreigners). This becomes reinforced by mama's and papa's reactions, who may remark, "They're not our kind" and "Stay away from such people." Incidentally, this poisonous attitude spills over to fraternities, sororities, country clubs, bridge clubs, and even churches. Incidentally, the growing child becomes highly sensitized to such names as "Wops," "Niggers," "Micks," "Chinks," "Krauts," "Heinies," and a host of other nomenclatures which verify such zenophobic behavior very readily. One's family consists of the "good guys" who are always right in their opinions of others, while the foreigners are "the bad guys" who pose continual threats by attempting to steal jobs away from "the good guys," or who attempt to degrade the family socially.

Siblings are prone to adopt parental teachings at home. They become sensitized to such stimuli (learning). This applies to religious beliefs, political trends, and almost all "knowledge" which these siblings absorb. Particularly threatening subjects are dwelt upon at length and strenuously, so that the believing siblings will become highly sensitized or hypersensitized to these specific problems and will react accordingly. A specific example is, "We don't want any Niggers living in our neighborhood, and we don't want any Niggers to enter as students in our private schools."

Hypersensitized parents can become somewhat deflated when new black neighbors arrive in a Mark IV with a chauffeur, and are highly intelligent, cultured, and well-dressed. The erstwhile hostiles might even shout, "Good morning", to their new black neighbors, particularly if the "colored" father is wearing an eagle or star on his Army or Marine uniform.

Perchance the Immunologic Theory "catches on" and survives the tides of argument as to its logic and usefulness to psychologists and psychiatrists. I will state categorically that before it does, many colleagues who are associated closely and currently with other schools of psychologic theory will put up battles to preserve their identities. Perhaps the main reason for such possible vehemence lies in the potential consequences of losing struggle. If forced to change their viewpoints, the situation could become highly painful to them; it usually is, when one is forced to forsake his pet beliefs under the onslaught of new knowledge. In other words, the objectors lose their security blankets: they will be forced to study the new knowledge and to change their cerebration on topics they had taken for granted throughout the years. Such is not an easy task, nor does it create a comfortable feeling.

Let me give you a simple example of such a turn of events which took place in the field of medicine. Puerperal or child-bed fever was rampant in many European clinics where mothers were delivered of their infants. The death rate from this disease was of staggering proportions. Doctors and medical students would leave the morgues and would deliver women without washing their hands thoroughly. Women and their offspring died at frightening rates until Dr. Ignaz Phillip Semmelweis (1818—65), a Hungarian, while in Vienna, insisted that all those who delivered babies should wash their hands carefully. The results from his teachings proved astounding, but produced wrath among those surgical colleagues who continued to oppose him. His two children passed away in infancy, and he was derided as "The Mad Jew" until finally this prolonged ecospheral trauma caused him to develop a psychosis.

This tragic example of new medical knowledge so unnerved his surgical confreres that he retreated finally to unreality because of his continued frustratory experiences which, in turn, caused him great pain intellectually (cortical hypersensitizations) and emotionally (subthalamic hypersensitizations). It takes a very strong personality to keep his equilibrium when confronted with such ecospheral onslaughts. We tend to forget that historic advancements in our knowledge have often been highly traumatic to their discoverers. People seem to object to changes. Laissez-faire appears to be the attitude of so many individuals. Similar emotional eruptions occur in other fields of endeavor. Musical audiences have rioted when new types of music were presented for the first time, as when "The Rite of Spring" was played for the first time by a symphony orchestra, conducted by Igor Stravinsky, the music's composer.

A few years ago, I wrote a paper which further explains the public's reaction upon the individual. Through the courtesy of the editors and publishers, it is presented here in full (1).

A Psychiatrist Raises the Devil

"Oh, shame to men! Devil with devil damned
Firm concord holds, men only disagree
of creatures rational."

Paradise Lost—Milton

It has always interested me to ascertain just why mankind has employed the Devil concept to explain certain behavior, rational or otherwise. It is not intended to make a comprehensive inquiry into the theologic aspects of this subject nor to pass judgment. An attempt will be presented to link the Devil concept to some aspects of anti-social human behavior from Freudian and psychoimmunologic constructs, with emphasis on the latter viewpoint, after making a short review of the etiology of Satan.

Probably from the beginning of mankind there have been "the good guys" versus "the bad guys." Perhaps this concept reached its peak in the western movies where "the good guys" or heroes wore white hats and their adversaries donned black hats. Simply stated, right usually prevailed over wrong, for the heroes usually vanquished their wary opponents, the villains, with great dispatch and with no little fanfare. Evidently, the moviegoing public enjoyed these spectacles immensely, for their previous religious education accentuated the inevitable outcome from such conflicts, which previously had been described in detail from countless pulpits throughout the land and abroad.

The origin of the Devil concept is interesting. Satan is

another name for the Devil. The Persian counterpart is Ahriman, who was the opponent of Ormuzd, or Ahura Mazda, the good one. This dualistic belief of good versus bad infiltrated Semitic philosophy, where the bad one tempted, accused, and punished those who had transgressed. These beliefs later permeated Christian thought, wherein the serpent became identified with the Devil or Satan. Obviously, this evil one became the enemy of God. Judeo-Christian theology, during the Middle Ages, began identifying the Devil as having the odor of brimstone; also he had cleft hoofs and a forked tail (2). Luther claimed that Satan plied his evil procedures so that the world would pass away with its pleasures, since no improvement could take place because of Satan's presence (3).

More recently, theologians have differed in their interpretations of the Devil. Some defend the biblical interpretation, while others have taken a more liberal approach. Belief in the Devil is not now essential to Christian doctrine, nor is it supposed to be indispensable in experiencing Christianity, according to modern Christian theology.

The Freudian View

Whether or not one accepts Freudian doctrine as the gospel, one must admit that, during the time of its formulation, no adequate personality theory existed. Later, this state was rectified by Piaget's brilliant studies of his children's development of their individual personalities.

Recently, I attempted to explain Freudian theorizing regarding personality development (4) in biologic terms. According to Freud, the Id originates certain crude forces that play upon the Ego, which in turn attempts to control the individual's behavior along more socially acceptable lines. The Superego, representing those forces emanating from one's environment (as from peers, parents, and teachers), also tend to check the final behavior of the Ego. In other words, the Superego functions as the individual's forces derived from parental and societal influences, and acts as the child's conscience and moral sense.

Perhaps you may recall TV star Flip Wilson's famed line, "The Devil made me do it." Unbridled impulses originating within the Id bear upon the Ego. Should the subsequent behavior of the individual prove to be more or less antisocial, then one may reason that such unbridled and asocial reactions were produced by uncontrollable Id impulses. Obviously, the Superego failed in its preventive or modulating reactions on the Ego.

A very simple way to explain this asocial behavior is through the rationalization that evil forces were at work within the Id. These spilled on to the Ego, and some nefarious actions ensued. In other words, the Devil did it; he was the cause. Here we return to the age-old concept of bad or evil versus good (righteousness). These are metaphysical concepts which cannot be related to behavioristic theory and physiologic functions. Hope, faith, and charity are similar metaphysical concepts which, apparently, have no counterparts in scientific terms. Apparently the same impasse exists in the case of Satan or the Devil. Not so, say I, and this is why.

Psychoimmunologic Approach

A previous reference (5) stated that Id force originated in the thalamic, subthalamic, and reticuloform bodies and was transmitted to the cerebral cortex, the sites of previous learning from encoding of the various afferent cortical cells from afferent stimuli. The latter can be regarded as the site of the Freudian Ego, and the ecosystem (stimuli originating from teachers, parents, and peers) can be regarded as the Superego. Obviously, learning in any individual is based upon certain neuroelectrochemical imprinting from afferent stimuli on the recipient cortical cells.

As has been stressed repeatedly by this writer, two types of afferent stimuli travel these neural pathways to the brain. It is important to differentiate pain-producing stimuli from those stimuli that do not produce pain (6). Stress was placed on the etiologic point that excessive painful stimuli can produce phobias, whereas excessive pleasurable stimuli tend to cause manias.

Hence, a hypersensitized thalamic or hypothalamic center may generate stimuli which finally produce either pleasurable or painful stimuli in the individual, and the resultant behavior can be regarded by those within one's ecosystem as being either socially acceptable or antisocially oriented. Reversing the character-producing processes: the individual reacts to his environment; then his parents, peers, or teachers observe his behavior, and his actions produce pain or pleasure or even a combination of both to these observers.

Reducing such physiologic reactions to philosophic terms, a person who produces socially acceptable behavior (resulting in pleasurable stimuli) is often regarded as a "good guy" or even a saint, whereas an individual who reacts antisocially (produces pain on his ecosystem) is thought as being possessed of the Devil. "Devilish" behavior originates from a hypersensitized subcortical area in the affected individual because of previously excessive cortical sensitizations (overlearning). His unwarranted behavior produces painful stimuli in those who are adjacent to such a hypersensitized individual. Such reactions can vary from disgust at to escape from further noxious stimuli from such a devilish person. In short, we have a physiologic explanation for those well known reactions which ensue when the "good guy" is pitted against the "bad guy."

"Why should the Devil have all the good tunes?"
—Rowland Hill

14

Sensitizations and

Hypersensitizations

In the preceding chapter, we considered some reactions of the enviornment on the individual. It should be emphasized that each person develops his own personality from his own environmental reactions. This interaction between the person and his environment is the matter of individual psychology. But when two or more persons are involved in living processes, the reactions ensuing between these individuals become the matter of social psychology. It often proves difficult to separate the individual from others since all are so interdependent: the warmth or the hostility of one affects others with whom he happens to be associated at the moment.

Since the study of immunology depends upon one's reaction to injury, it becomes apparent that an individual's personality will be heavily dependent upon the general nature of his environment. Is it generally hostile and pain producing, or is it generally pleasure producing? The individual, because of Darwin's law of self-preservation, responds in a much more favorable way to the latter type of environment. So with his uninterrupted maturation, without the deficits excessive coldness and hunger are capable of producing, he tends to become a more friendly individual. If he is forced to fight continually for, his own survival, he tends to become a hostile, unfriendly person. This has been shown to be the case with youngsters who have been raised in slum areas, where one's mere survival might be marginal and even life-threatening. Proper education is at a minimum in such impoverished sections of urban life. Hence, this lad will find it very difficult to compete with others who are raised in economically plentiful sections, where the attainment of each meal is assured. Being wanted and loved are essential also for normal life. A person who resides in a backward rural area (1) might be expected to react differently from those who eke out existences in teeming, congested urban slum areas.

It is obvious that totally different types of stimuli from divergent ecosystemal origins produce totally different behavioral reactions in people. Although the African bushman hunts game as does the Eskimo, their hunting procedures differ markedly, as do their modes of dress, food habits, and personalities. Each individual must learn to avoid the dangers that exist in the particular ecosystem in which he lives. If the Eskimo resides in an environment free from tribal wars and fierce competition, he does not mind sharing his woman with strangers who visit his community. The bushman in Africa might have to remain aware continually of other tribesmen who carry on warlike activities. Obviously he will regard strangers with suspicion and even hostility if he feels that his survival is endangered. He will show xenophobic behavior to most outsiders. In summary, we can state that pain-producing environmental stimuli tend to make individuals who reside in unpleasant areas more or less hostile. Those who live in a more or less pleasure-producing (nonpainful) area tend to be friendly. Their normal maturation will probably be less impeded as the years pass, particularly if serious deprivations do not occur.

The reader should remember that personal esteem is an important means whereby each individual can take heed of how he stands in his own opinion. It represents, at a given time in his life span, the results of his battles with his environment. As you may recall, his personal esteem might be at a high level if he has been able to win most of his environmental (ecosystemal) battles. His personal esteem may become reversed if the opposite occurs. Obviously, his personal esteem will soar if he happens to win a Nobel Prize, and it might be at a very low ebb if he happens to flunk out of school.

When social psychologists speak of social and cultural factors, they are in reality, talking about ecosystemal stimuli such as we have already discussed. One's particular personality can be considered as resulting from the behavioral changes which have taken place in the individual in consequence of his continual environmental battles. A pleasant personality is fashioned in a person mainly because of his residing in a pleasure-producing environment, while a hostile type of personality usually results from a pain-evoking environment.

It is important for the reader to remember that each individual's behavior is the end result of his environment plus his inherited characteristics, such as biologic weaknesses and strengths, exemplified by the strength or frailty of the bodily (anatomical) and physiologic structuring of an individual's inherited properties (through his familial genes). His environmental forces play upon him continually. In spite of these forces, which may be pleasure or pain-producing, if he can maintain some semblance of homeostasis he may well emerge as a dominant personality. Or he may become depressed—weakened emotionally and physically—if he has difficulty in establishing homeostasis (2).

All of the above is involved in the genesis of one's personality. But this genesis is complicated by social aspects that form important ecosystemal factors. There is continual give and take among one's parents, siblings, peers at school and social groups. Ecosystemic forces are at play constantly that affect each individual even while attending church. Splits in church congregations have occurred because of the myriads of differences in people brought about by what they had learned and had accepted. The extent of differentiation swells markedly as we consider all the individual differences which can be found in cities, counties, states, and countries.

All these individual differences are further compounded when we consider international differences. If economic pressures affect a majority of citizens in one country sufficiently to make their lives too painful, they may seek relief through warlike behavior. Thus, the Arabs want the return of lands taken by the Israelis, who, in turn, want to keep this land gained from previous battles as a buffer against possible future Arab aggressions. Think of all the hypersensitized hypothalami that are sending pain-producing sensations in these war torn lands and throughout the world. The Arabs own oil. Many nations need it! What a mess!

My students have been asked if they truly believe that mankind is capable of maintaining peace through the United Nations or other peace-keeping procedures. The answer seems quite obvious. If family members are unable to reside together in peace, how can nations do so?

The individual's problems concern the therapist in clinical psychology or psychiatry. The many ills of mankind in their social context concern diplomats and sociologists. If these agencies for peace do not succeed, then mankind again might become engulfed in legalized mass killings!

We are supposedly intelligent, rational human beings. Yet pain-producing ecosystemic stimuli can hypersensitize us to the point of irrational hostility. What then happens to all man's knowledge and culture? Nations, when they become warlike, throw steel and lead at their adversaries, not music: homo *sap*iens is our name!

Modus Operandi for Immunologic Psychology

What follows is an outline of the main events produced by the environmental stimuli that play continually upon each human being. The drawing summarizes the chain of events

that follow the application of ecosystemal energies on individuals. One's general character and behavior are dependent upon just how his environment affects him and whether
or not he can cope with it satisfactorily through the attempts
at homeostasis that follows each injury resulting from pain
producing stimuli. The genesis of these events should prove
to be easily understood from the following construct for
explaining behavior.

CORPUS OF THE IMMUNOLOGIC THEORY (3)

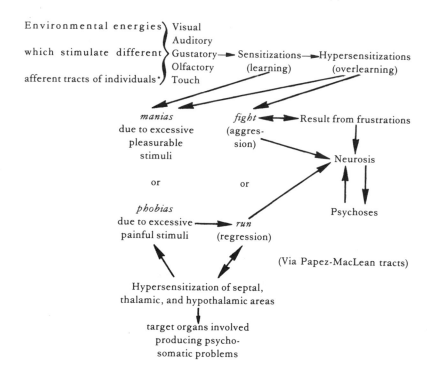

*Includes one's peers, teachers, parents and entire environment which engulf
each individual continually. All of these stimuli-producing sources perpetually play
upon each individual who can be overwhelmed by this particular environment (good
or bad) during his lifetime, unless he can escape to a more friendly ecosystem.

15

Diagnostic Psychology
Procedures

The immunologic approach is similar to a musical composition that employs a simple theme as the basic structure upon which variations are written, followed by returns to the basic theme. The author hopes his readers and students will employ a similar procedure with our theory to explain the many variations found in human behavior. These have been found to be quite understandable after someone has enunciated the basic themes. I am sure that further variations of the Immunologic Theory have yet to be written. What follows is but another example of immunologic variations on the basic theme.

Word Association Tests

As the allergist employs scratch tests to determine what specific substances produce hypersensitivity in his patients, so do word association tests help to discover which subjects have produced learning hypersensitivities.

After the allergist has scarified the patient's skin, he rubs into the scratches small amounts of substances that can produce redness and swelling in skin areas which reacted to the allergens (pollen, food, dermal, etc. extracts). Itching frequently affects these skin areas that contain the sensitizing material to which the subject reacts abnormally.

Similarly, the psychologist prepares a list of names of objects. Some of these items might be connected with painful past episodes experienced by that patient. Other words will act as fill-ins. The patient then reads the word lists and writes the first word which comes to him, or the examiner might read the list and have the patient give the very first word which the patient recalls. It has been known for years that certain key words can produce emotional reactions in such hypersensitized patients. For example, a man killed his rival with a Colt revolver as the result of an argument over an unfaithful wife. When given a list of words to respond to, he said "blood" for the word red, and "shoot" for revolver, "hate" for rival, and so on. He was overreacting to these key words in the word list, but his reactions to the other non-essential words were given in a normal manner. In other words, he responded to the subjects to which he had become hypersensitized. In a quite similar fashion, the allergist who performs skin (scratch) tests determines what allergens have produced overreactions (hypersensitizations) in his allergic patient.

A series of tests similar to the time-honored word association tests are based upon the G.S.R. (Galvanic Skin Response) or the Psychogalvanic Reflex (P.G.R.). This equipment directly records skin potentials (electric current increases) which are caused by the patient's emotional responses to certain key words. This is quite similar to the older word association tests with the exception that the examiner can record directly the patient's autonomic changes which take place whenever he encounters the key words. Thus, the G.S.R., the respiratory rate, the blood pressure, and the heart (pulse) rate are recorded simultaneously on recording paper by equipment which had been attached to the patient. It is known that the triggering of emotional reactions sets off increases of sweat, which serves as a good conductor for an electrical impulse in the skin. The answers given by a patient being examined by the so-called "lie detector" are noted, and when an excessive reaction occurs to questions that contain key words, the equipment picks this up with a marked increased galvanic skin response. Hence, this procedure can detect hypersensitized states in the individual being tested; and this form of testing can, to a more or less degree, determine whether the patient's answers are truthful. The only drawbacks with this procedure are that this test cannot differentiate between the lies of a guilty party and the intense fear engendered in an innocent person. (1) However, an expert with this equipment can determine, to a high degree, whether or not the patient is responding truthfully to the examiner's questions.

With the word association tests, the patient reacts to his cerebral and subcortical states of hypersensitivity, because of the excessive afferent stimuli which produced such hypersensitivity from what he sees and hears. The examiner introduces items that are intimately connected with the patient's hypersensitized states. Fill-in words do not set off emotional responses, but words associated with hypersensitizing learned states have the capacity to trigger emotional reactions that dump into the autonomic nervous system to increase blood pressure, pulse rate, rate of respiration, and galvanic skin response.

A similar feedback of acquired data (knowledge) occurs whenever a teacher tests students. Previously, the student had sensitized his recipient cerebral centers to the flow of afferent stimuli that had acquainted him with his environment, which, in this case, was from books he had read and from the teacher's speech. Thus, in the first instance the student's uncinate (cerebral) areas stored data from the afferent pathways connected with sight. The teacher's lectures, verbal illustrations, sensitized the pupil's temporal (cerebral) areas to what he heard. Such brain encoding, with its storage because of the many neuroelectrochemical brain cell changes, constituted his receipt of what we consider to be knowledge.

Then the teacher samples the storage and retrieval (via the Leyden Jar principle) of this data and thereby assigns a grade to the student's answers. But if the student became *hypersensitized* to any particular cerebral encoding, an excessive verbal or behavioral response could well ensue. The student might stomp from the room, or he might yell through his disgust (excessive emotional reaction) or even destroy the exam paper. There are various ways such a student might react whenever his hypersensitized state happens to be tapped.

Similar situations abound in everyday life to such previous hypersensitizations because of what one perceives from one or more of his five afferent neural tracts to the brain's recording centers. For example, a friend of mine was cautioned repeatedly that the time for paying his taxes was nigh. He became hypersensitized to the concept of having to pay taxes. His financial status was precarious, to say the least. So when I happened to mention that today was the last day for paying taxes, he "hit the ceiling" by exploding verbally and emotionally about the subject. Others do not usually react to the subject of taxes so vehemently. But whenever persons become hypersensitized to particular subjects because of previous associated and excessive aural or visual stimuli, they too overreact to such additional stimuli which are related, as I have stated repeatedly, to whether or not previous related stimuli have hypersensitized his cerebral encoding centers.

Other psychologic tests appear to operate quite similarly. For example, the Rorschach Test employs ten symmetrical ink splotches, which the patient examines via his visual tracts. These cards act as visual stimuli, and he might react to one or more of these ink spots in an unusual manner, particularly if a card unlocks a memory that had produced hypersensitization to that subject.

The Thematic Apperception Test (TAT) views certain stimulus pictures made for younger or older men or women. Again, what they view tends to set off autonomic or motor reactions, particularly if the picture they see hits a previously hypersensitized state, and then the subject responds accordingly.

It is not within this scope of this volume to examine all the various tests that are available for psychologic testing. However, readers who consult Freedman and Kaplan's textbook (2) will find a highly satisfactory review of what each of these tests accomplishes.

In summary, one can only test for data that learning produces, stores, and retrieves within the afferent recipient centers of the brain (cerebration). One cannot assimilate knowledge unless the above three cerebral processes can function. Nor can this acquired data (knowledge) be tapped and measured by any means unless these same processes are able to function. These various tests merely give a token sampling of what the individual's brain has recorded. Testing is quite similar to dipping a calibrated yardstick into a gas tank to determine how much gas is present in the tank. The yardstick does not determine the octane of the gas. But if for some unexplained reason the gas tank cap flies off because of excessive pressure, similarly to what happens when one's radiator becomes overheated for some unknown reason and the radiator explodes, we realize that such reactions are not normal. Similarly, when a patient is given a stimulus to which he had been hypersensitized previously, the "tank cap" might be blown off by the excessive emotional reaction engendered by the hypersensitized stimuli which the examiner has introduced unwarily.

Many years ago, it was discovered that most of the bodily organs performed specific functions. Tests were devised by internists and clinical pathologists for some of these specific functions. Hence, there are specific functional tests for the liver, pancreas, stomach, heart, etc. The human brain also has specific functions, and these are tested to determining just how well each function works. Some of the psychologic tests we have described serve one purpose better than another. But the most important point is that we should know as much as possible about each function we desire to test, about the physiology and the anatomy of the organ whose function we desire to sample. The diagnosis of other bodily and nervous disorders is predicated upon similar logic.

We may also append that we would not expect abnormal reactions to occur when a patient is tested with psychologic procedures unless he happens to be harboring states of hypersensitivity as the result of excessive psychoimmunogens (psychoantigens) which may have brought about such hypersensitivity during the process of learning. We would expect reactions embodying normal responses to such psychologic testing if the previous cerebral encoding was within normal limits. Hypersensitivity of the cerebral encoding centers can produce abnormal responses to psychologic testing should an afferent stimulus be introduced which is related to his hypersensitized state brought about through what my old teacher, Clark Hull, termed overlearning (hypersensitizing reaction).

16

Immunologic
Interpretation of
Therapies *

Various modern therapeutic modalities used for psychologic and psychiatric therapy may seem unrelated. The purpose of this chapter is to demonstrate that these various therapeutic methods possess common bonds.

A viable and uncomplicated basic theory might assist decidely to explain the etiologic aspects which have to do with these various therapies. Hence, a brief review of the immunologic approach will be presented which may explain normal as well as abnormal behavior.

If we recall it correctly, the "association of ideas" theory was first mentioned in Plato's *The Republic*. About 200 years ago an English physician, Dr. David Hartley (1705-57), introduced a rather remarkable concept that sensory stimuli reach the human brain by means of tiny vibrations which her terms "vibruncules." It is known that Sir Isaac Newton (1704) wrote along similar lines. Both authors mentioned the "association of ideas" theory (2) which was concerned with thinking, reasoning, and remembering—all contributed markedly to early psychological theory.

---

*Based on a 1973 article by the author (1). I am grateful to the editors and publishers for allowing its reproduction. The data on acupuncture has been added. The article was written to be self-sufficient, since its typical readers would be physicians who had at least a potential interest in immunologic theory.

Dr. David Hartley had a famed student named Joseph Priestley (1733-1804), who received a Doctorate of Laws degree from the University of Edinburgh. Dr. Priestley not only gained lasting fame through his discovery of oxygen, but he also identified a large group of other gases not then known. He wrote a volume on Dr. Hartley's "association of ideas" (3), and some of his data were mentioned in one of my papers (4). Then James Mill (1773-1836), his brilliant son, John Stuart Mill (1806-1872), and some of their colleagues further expounded Dr. Hartley's theory on the "Association of ideas." (4). However, these early psychological teachings lost their vogue with the passage of time, and are now mentioned chiefly in relation to the history of philosophy.

Doctors Hartley and Priestley advocated that the incoming (afferent) stimuli encoded the human cerebrum, although during their times the nature of neural impulses was not known. As Dr. Priestley wrote, the newborn brain is similar to a blank sheet of white paper. But as the effects of sensations infringe upon the brain, the results from afferent sensations are received in the brain, retained (memory), and employed to create ideas of association, whenever identical neural impulses are received by the brain. This was a decided forward step for our modern knowledge relating to cerebration.

Basis for Immunologic Theory

What follows is a synopsis for the immunologic approach to behavior. As Hartley and Priestley stated, the effects from sensory perception, via the touch, smell, taste, visual and auditory tracts, are encoded or recorded in the recipient and cerebral centers. There they are stored as memory because of resultant neuroelectro-chemical changes in the cerebral cells. Hartley and Priestley spoke of these memory traces as ideas which are associated with further incoming afferent impulses of similar nature. Here the phenomenon of recall takes place, for the individual recalls the previous sensitizing effects through the receipt of similar or related afferent stimuli through the functioning of the neural discharges possibly emanating from a Leyden jar-like process.

However, we term these incoming afferent stimuli as psychoantigens or psychoimmunogens, which can sensitize the recipient cortical centers. This process really serves as the basis for learning since these encoded brain areas contain added brain potentials which can be released through one's recognition of associated psychoantigens which happen to be incoming at these cerebral centers. This constitutes memory and its resultant recall. This process is also important for one's intellectual creativity, as Arthur Koestler has written (6).

The introduction of psychoantigens follows the more-or-less law, because their dosage strengths, the nature of the afferent tracts involved, the time factor, and whether or not previous related psychoantigens have encoded the cerebral cells, all play important roles in the imprinting of these cortical cells from environmental sources through the individual's afferent neural tracts.

There appear to be additional important factors which will tend to sensitize or even hypersensitize these recipient cortical cells. Whether all this results in *pain inducing* or *pleasure inducing* stimuli seems highly important. If such stimuli tend to produce pain, their effects tend to be more marked on the cerebral encoding process, and hypersensitization of such cerebral areas may well ensue. This appears to be quite similar to the Hullian concept which involves overlearning. Frustration can become associated with such a process, and the individual will either run (regression) or fight (aggression) according to the well-known Darwinian concept.

These cortical encoded areas (containing information) can be considered as not merely being sensitized or even hypersensitized, but as containing electrical potentials which are not present until after the cerebral imprinting occurs. So these electrically involved cortical areas act similar to tiny Leyden jars, since they store these electric potentials which result from cerebral encoding from afferent stimuli. After further excessive sensitizations of a particular nature become stored, the cerebral area's maximal ability to hold such potentials may spill over (surmenage) via the Papez-MacLean circuitry to the septal, thalamic, and the hypothalamic areas which also tend to become hypersensitized. If such a process is continued without abatement, then the target organs of the body may become involved to produce psychosomatic difficulties (7) through the autonomic nervous system, which then sensitizes or even hypersensitizes these affected organs (i.e., various gastric upsets, bronchospasms, certain cutaneous changes, as with the neurodermatoses).

Psychologic and Psychiatric Therapies

A comprehensive volume could be written on this topic. It is important to remember that psychologic and psychiatric therapies are based on the fundamental theory that pain can be produced by frustrations of various types. These frustrations (reviewed by us (8)) usually are caused by painful experiences, many of which tend to become supposedly suppressed in the Freudian subconscious. We cannot subscribe to this point, since the so-called subconscious is only a philosophical entity used to explain the inability of a patient's recall process. Prolonged associative techniques are used to free these temporarily suppressed thoughts with the use of various techniques including psychoanalysis. According to the immunologic theory, these repressed bits of information are released through the use of desensitizing procedures. These involve the introduction of infinitesimal amounts of related psychoimmunogens which tend to build up the patient's ability to cope with his hypersensitized state, similarly to the allergist's treatment of disorders which had previously hypersensitized patients to noxious substances, such as pollens, rusts, molds, smuts, etc. These allergic substances are gradually introduced until the allergic patient does not react chemically or clinically to them. The psychoanalyst gradually increases the dosage of irritating concepts which had produced the patient's withdrawal from noxious psychic stimuli. These regressive states become less painful as such therapy proceeds. However, if these painful psychoimmunogens are introduced too rapidly or in too strong doses, the patient may relapse into a markedly depressed state (withdrawal from reality-regression) and may even commit suicide, which can be considered as the ultimate stage of complete frustration.

The time honored Wier-Mitchell Therapy for psychiatric disorders was simple and to the point. This therapist merely removed the hypersensitized mental patient from his irritating and pain producing environment by placing him in the new and pleasant environment until the patient rested sufficiently to return to his former painful ecosphere. This form of therapy was similar to putting a hypersensitized patient to ragweed out of a ragweed patch into a new environment free from such irritating pollen antigens. The patient took a boat ride where ragweed was not present or the patient travelled to a Canadian area free from these irritating pollens until frost killed the pollen bearing plants in his home area.

Pearson (9) wrote:

> Sometimes the therapist takes a treatment leaf from the practice of the allergist, who may desensitize patients by injecting small doses of the pollen or other offending material. The therapist may practice psychological desensitization...Before the therapist attempts psychological desensitization, he should have good understanding of the nature of the underlying conflict and of the personality of the patient. Furthermore, he should note carefully the

reaction, and increase or decrease desensitizing dose accordingly... To desensitize successfully, the therapist must have and give out confidence. Uncertainty is contagious and fatal. Here again, the therapist is the strong, dependable father from whom stability and emotional security are derived.

Pearson did not explain how sensitization and hypersensitization occurred. Others recently have jumped on the bandwagon with their therapeutic use of desensitization. For example, Wolpe employs similar desensitizing procedures which he has termed reciprocal inhibition. Small amounts of afferent stimuli, associated with the patient's hypersensitivities, are introduced until the patient doesn't respond abnormally. For instance, a child afraid of snakes is very slowly brought in small increments, to a pet boa constrictor, until he is able to pet the serpent. This is psychologic desensitization, which one of us discussed before the American Psychological Association's Annual meeting at Ohio State University, circa 1938. In other words, the therapist attempts to substitute pleasurable for erstwhile painful stimuli, which were caused many times by multiple frustrations.

Because psychoanalysis may take years, many neo-Freudians have attempted to streamline their procedure, since the original method also is usually exceedingly expensive. The main proponent for this newer procedure was Franz Alexander (10). These therapies are methods for relieving explosive psychic (neuro-electro-chemical) potentials by allowing the patient to decompress himself by "talking out" these problems. Thus, the pressures created by these excessive sensitizations or hypersensitizations are allowed to become dissipated. This is usually accomplished in a quiet atmosphere free from additional pain-producing psychoimmunogens so that homeostasis can occur.

Milieu therapy appears to serve the same purpose of

placing the emotionally disturbed patient in a more pleasant surrounding where he can be protected against further painful stimuli. One might consider this form of therapy as being a take-off from the time honored Wier-Mitchell therapy where the patient is entirely removed from the noxious environmental stimuli which have caused him much pain. Obviously, one cannot remain indefinitely in such artificial and more or less pleasurable surroundings, because there always comes the time when the patient must return to his erstwhile environment with its pain-producing tendencies. However, the rest periods obtained by these therapies might allow him to establish homeostatic reactions which will tend to bolster his innate defense mechanisms. In other words, the passage of time, and his desensitization (being free from further pain producing stimuli), will help the person's healing processes similarly as going away on a vacation will avoid the pain-producing stimuli from the patient's particular painful ecosystem.

Behavioral Therapy

Watson, during the 20's, was possibly the best known advocate for the behavioral system, although at present there are variations of this technique of therapy. Krech states that this treatment is based on conditioning. Whenever an undesirable symptom occurs in a patient, a painful stimulus is applied to bring the symptom under control through relaxation and desensitization procedures. Here again, the results from previous frustrations produce painful situations in patients. Desensitization is attempted by employing similar pain-producing stimuli in small amounts until the patient can cope with the situation. We fail to comprehend why such therapy is termed conditioning, since the procedure really resembles the same technique used in desensitizing patients who have become hypersensitized to allergens or immunogens.

The same argument applies to the so-called client-centered therapy. With this treatment, the therapist desensitizes the patient to whatever problems the patient has produced through what he has said or how he acts. The patient does not know why he shows abnormal behavior, and it becomes the therapist's task to explain to the patient the reasons behind such behavior so that the patient will comprehend finally the causes for his difficulties. Again, we can consider this type of therapy as a form of desensitization. In other words, the therapist attempts to rid the patient of his untoward effects which have resulted from pain inducing stimuli.

Learning Theories

These psychotherapies use various learning theories (11). The basis for such therapy makes sense because some abnormal forms of learning must have occurred which produced painful episodes in these patients. As was mentioned, frustrations can occur from learning episodes as pain producing stimuli are conveyed to and encoded in the individual's cerebral cortex and his subcortical centers. These painful experiences result usually from conflicts involving social learning. In other words, these painful episodes originate from a pain producing ecosystem. Pain cannot result from ecosystems which are pleasurable to an individual. It is important to remember that people certainly form major parts of one's ecosystem unless he happens to live alone on an isolated island. The obvious approach to this type of psychotherapy is for the therapist to substitute non-painful procedures for treating a pain-scarred patient. Physicians use this basic procedure when they treat a pain-racked patient with medications which alleviate pain. As the therapist allows his patient to discuss his problems, desensitization may slowly take place, so that finally the patient gains sufficient insight into his erstwhile problems so that discussions of these former painful episodes do not bother him enough to upset his equilibrium.

Obviously, re-educative therapy attempts to substitute pleasurable stimuli and attempts to have the patient avoid further pain producing stimuli. Also, such therapy substitutes normally functioning neural tracts and their cerebral encoding centers to replace defective neural counter parts. A well known example was the case of Helen Keller, whose auditory and optic tracts became deficient in infancy. Her functional olfactory gustatory, and neural tracts were employed to introduce information derived from her environment which became encoded in her recipient cortical centers.

The Desensitization Therapy of a Puppy

Years ago, when the performance of house calls was commonplace by physicians, I made house calls on one particular family, not alone to treat the ill children in this one family, but also to play with their beautiful cocker spaniel puppy, who showed his affection by voiding on my shoes and pants.

This family lived next door to a school. The school children would abuse the puppy by throwing stones and hitting him with sticks. In a short time this puppy, by the name of Frisky, became quite hostile (hypersensitized) since he snapped and growled at his tormentors. Finally, the family was forced to get rid of this unfortunate dog. They asked if I wanted Frisky and I accepted him with much fervor. However, no one could go near his cage because he continued to snarl even when I tried to feed him. The pup had to be taught to play.

After a time, with love and affection, he allowed me to hand him food. He was allowed in our home and he immediately took over my favorite arm chair as his private property. He would glare at us, but it wasn't too long before our affection for Frisky began to show dividends. He continued to snarl whenever anyone approached him with a stick. He became gentle and affectionate and remained so until his death, which was due to a heart attack during a particularly hot summer day ten years later.

The Darwinian concept of fight or run had been demonstrated amply. Excessive painful incidents (with frustration) will inevitably produce such behavior in beasts and man. Remove the painful stimuli and recovery can take place. Such appears to be the basis for most forms of psychotherapy.

Various Group Therapies

These methods were evolved to save time and money. Groups of patients are treated collectively rather than singly. Also, group therapy, some believe, is more life-like and real than is individual therapy. We doubt if this form of treatment is superior to the older method with individual therapy because there may be a multiplication of personality clashes which may add to present conflicts rather than deplete them. The basis for adequate psychotherapy should be the lessening of painful sensitizations of patients. Obviously, this cannot be controlled adequately when multiple patients become involved.

There are many forms of group therapy such as encounter groups, T-groups, sensitivity groups, etc. Some investigations of these therapies differ in their ideas concerning group therapy, where the patient's loneliness is supposedly lost with group activity. However, added psychic damage (due to further painful incidents) might easily do more damage than good.

Family Therapy

This therapeutic procedure of treating the patient's family makes much sense. When the patient (who has been psychically injured) returns to his family life, the members of the family attempt at least to understand the patient's problems and avoid further pain-producing conflicts. This is all well and good when the family members cooperate. But when the opposite occurs, then the patient finds himself in his previous painful environment and his trouble may return.

Psychodrama

Here the patient "acts out" his psychic difficulties, thereby allowing himself to become desensitized to some degree. This procedure is not a complete panacea in itself, although it allows him to see himself as others might view him. Certainly more data on this form of therapy is needed.

Play Therapy

This method is employed with children who find the therapist to be a kindly person who tends to protect them from additional pain.

Other Types

Some of these are a bit far-fetched such as those groups who hold hands, practice nudism, and what have you! They do not appear to be worthy of further consideration at present. They seem to dote on the false idea that the world and the people in it were made for love. How silly can one get?

Psychiatric Therapies

Many forms of psychiatric therapy have come and gone. Among these were Metrazol, insulin, histamine (introduced by the author and further studied by Sakel and Sakel) which were various forms of shock therapy. A similar type of therapy is electroshock (E.C.T.), which is employed currently and mainly for deep depressions.

Psychosurgery, especially lobotomy, was made popular by Freeman and Watts, in the '40s. Currently, newer approaches to brain surgery, mainly to control patient hostilities, has been in the news. For a provocative review of this topic, see Holden's review (13) of surgical techniques used to attack various parts of the limbic system. These are forms of so-called psychosurgery which are employed to change behavior through changes in the thought and emotion producing centers. Some critics claim that such psychosurgical procedures constitute threats to the future social control of certain low economy groups in the country.

Some forms of stereotactic psychosurgery introduce electrodes into the diseased portions of brains. The electrical current destroys these areas, thereby altering certain forms of violent behavior. Some of these newer surgical approaches are thalamotomy, cingulumotomy, and amygdalotomy, depending upon the exact subcortical nuclei which are attacked. At best, these forms of psychosurgery are in a state of flux, so far as their critics and supporters are concerned. Some court test cases are now on tap.

All physicians are well acquainted with the various phenothiazines and associated psychotropic medications. Although the exact sites of action are not known at present for many of these drugs, some affect the cerebral cortex, the septal regions, and the thalamic and subthalamic nuclei. The main therapeutic effects appear to be a dulling of those centers involving the thought processes and the emotion producing areas. In other words, and according to the immunologic concept, the erstwhile hypersensitized areas are temporarily controlled by causing them to become less sensitive to further incoming noxious stimuli. Pavlov might have termed this the inhibition of these centers.

Summary

The therapist's main role with treatment has been and continues to be the alleviation of pain produced by disorders of the psyche or soma (14). All behavior appears to be dependent upon afferent neural impulses which can sensitize the brain in varied amounts. The length of time these various stimuli operate is important as are their dosages and whether or not the individual has been sensitized to them previously. Excessive psychoimmunogens (afferent stimuli) can hypersensitize these recipient cortical centers in the process of encoding the brain. Additional similar neural stimuli tend to spill over (surmenage) from the cortical areas and may hypersensitize the septal, thalamic, and subthalamic regions. The usual Darwinian behavioral response is for the individual to fight (aggression) or to run (regression). These responses are produced by frustratory reactions which tend to enhance further stages of hypersensitivity in the affected areas.

Summarizing the many psychologic and psychiatric therapies and their modus operandi, the main therapeutic thrust appears to be aimed at the further prevention of pain-producing stimuli from causing added hypersensitized states in the already saturated cortical and subcortical areas. Presently, the therapeutic modalities have been concerned mainly with further pain prevention. The proper control of pain allows the individual more adequate time for attempts at homeostatic changes which favor normalcy. Proper therapeutic results are desired, no matter what form of therapy is employed by the therapist. The end result for therapy should be patient improvement through the amelioration of pain-producing situations with the various present therapeutic modalities.

Tan, Tan, and Vieth (15) describe acupuncture in their new and interesting book. They mention that this procedure was claimed by opponents of this therapy for pain as being effective through hypnosis or suggestion. Tan, Tan, and Vieth emphasize that infants and animals cannot be hypnotized, yet Chinese needle procedures are valuable for such therapy. They point out that Mongolian and Tibetal nomads have caused pain reduction in their horses for centuries.

Acupuncture, they claim, is employed in many psychogenic and emotional disabilities. They state that other western investigators believe acupuncture affects the thalamus, while Chinese workers in the field of acupuncture believe the hypothalamus, thalamus, and cortex are affected by this procedure.

Since the entry of the needles does not follow known neurologic anatomy, many western scientists have scoffed at these results from acupuncture. Be that as it may, much more must be learned about this mysterious procedure before it can be written off as ineffective for pain control.

An important principle should not be neglected by the reader. Perhaps the following fable will illustrate my point amply (16). When several of my colleagues read it, their reactions to what I believed was a humorous anecdote surprised me. One confrere thought it was a slur on other psychologists. But another insisted that it be included in the book. A professor of chemistry became convulsed with laughter, which shows one cannot predict just how people will react at times.

The Parable of the Gum Ball Machine

Once upon a time three learned psychologists decided they would enjoy some chewing gum. They spotted a gum ball machine down the corridor in their building. One of them followed directions on the machine and dutifully deposited his penny in the coin slot. Almost instantaneously a beautiful red ball of gum rolled into the receptacle. Another in the group then deposited his penny in the machine slot, and out popped a beautiful yellow ball of gum. Then the last member deposited his penny. He waited and waited for his gum ball with keen anticipation, but, alas! nothing happened.

They began discussing the situation, at first calmly, then most vociferously. Then they pounded on the machine and finally in desperation began to kick the machine's stand. Still no gum appeared. They began to swear. As they shook the machine with all of their might, they shouted some four letter words which might have shocked the dean.

Just then, a kindly old man appeared who seemed to understand their plight. Carefully, but swiftly and skillfully, he disassembled the machine. He smiled as he returned the penny. As he left them and walked down the hall he was heard to whistle softly "I can't give you anything but love, baby." A dog in a nearby room happened to overhear the conversation as he was running a maze. He stopped, thought for a while as he scratched his ear with his paw, then yapped "yep!"

The point of the fable seems obvious. One cannot perform proper therapeutic procedures until he recognizes what produced the malfunctioning. Remove the cause and adequate therapeutic results may follow. Here is an example.

A few days ago I was requested to see a young man in the hospital, because he had run away the day before I saw him. He had been confined to a hospital room which had its windows screened and its door locked. It was soon discovered that the patient was suffering from claustrophobia. He could not stand to be so confined in a room locked up. So he escaped from the room as soon as he could, and ran away from the hospital.

Upon further questioning, it was discovered that, during his early childhood, he was playing in his back yard, and a dump truck unloaded a truckful of sand and nearly buried him alive. From that time on, he avoided any sort of an environment which confined his movements. The patient never had related these reactions to his childhood experience, and a thorough explanation helped considerably in treating his phobia.

17

Pros and Cons

of Theory

Formation*

One of the first lectures I give my students is to explain the differences between theory, hypothesis, and law. These differentiations are important if a student is to become effective in his reactions to the data that he receives as he progresses with his studies in psychology.

While studying psychology, he meets with various concepts of learning, the basis for behavior. He meets with various explanations for the many psychologic phenomena. He should be able to differentiate between those theories which seem more or less realistic, logical, and scientific.

Many departments of psychology favor one or more schools of thought. But each student should become well acquainted with at least the major theories. Then he should be able to choose wisely as to the particular theory or theories which make the most sense to him.

There is decided interest currently in education and its possible upgrading. As learning forms the basis for education, appropriate learning techniques of a practical and even scientific nature are being suggested. A learning theory

---

*One of the first articles I wrote for my colleagues in medicine and for my students may supply the reader with sufficient data so that he can differentiate between a strong and a weak theory. Through the courtesy of the editors and publisher of *The Journal of the Medical Association of the State of Alabama,* the article is presented in its entirety (1).

which could explain both normal and abnormal behavior would be a decided boon. It would preferably be biologically oriented so that the various disciplines concerned with learning procedures could employ similar terminologies. Perhaps much mysticism, at present associated with psychodynamic approaches, might disappear, with an attendant clarification of the muddy waters that involve the human "mind."

Education, per se, should not be regarded as a complete panacea for all of mankind's problems, any more than psychiatry can be expected to eradicate all behavioral illnesses. Such emotionally provoked reactions as lust, hostility, greed, and a host of other antisocial reactions might be rechanneled to more socially acceptable lines, although the results from undesired human emotions have plagued mankind since its genesis and perhaps will continue so long as the human race exists. It is asking too much from education to completely change such untoward emotional reactions.

It might be expedient to review what are known as hypotheses, theories, and laws. One should know what can be expected from them. Equipped with this information, one may be in a much stronger position to discuss such topics intelligently.

Our knowledge of the molecular approach to learning, memory, and thinking is rather new. Few adequate scientific studies were available merely twenty years ago. In a paper published in 1969, I mentioned some of these highly interesting findings from the immunologic, neurophysiologic, and biochemical sources in their attempts to unravel the mysteries of the brain's functionings, which are still enshrouded in psychodynamic theories (2).

One distinguished psychiatrist (3) believes that fundamental investigations should be distinguished from clinical procedures, since the former have not as yet proven practical for the latter field. Perhaps this viewpoint is due to the lack of a suitable molecular theory for learning which can be applied to clinical psychiatry. One of the present tasks of this writer is to present the psychoimmunologic approach to explain certain clinical subjects biologically. Hence, it seems proper to consider at this point what a theory, hypothesis, or law is and what such should be expected from each.

The term "science" is defined by Dorland (4) as an "accumulating body of knowledge, especially that which seeks to establish general laws connecting a number of particular facts." Pure science is "concerned with the discovery of known laws relating to particular facts," while a law is defined as "a constant fact or principle." (5)

A theory (6) is defined as a speculation or even a contemplation or an analysis of a certain set of facts related to one another. A theory should enunciate a plausible general principle to explain a certain train of events in a systematic, clear, and sensible manner.

Braithwaite (7) states that a science functions by formulating the behavior of empirical events which concern science and connects them so that the prediction of events can be formulated. This same authority states that a hypothesis is "a general proposition about all the things of a certain sort." (8) The reader is referred to Braithwaite's book for a fuller discussion of this philosophical approach to a true theory based upon the use of common sense and adequate reasoning.

Many scientists believe: the simpler the theory, the stronger it may be. Given a theory based on multiple tenets, compared to one based upon simplicity, most workers will favor the latter. All are concerned with data supplied from scientific investigations to explain some principle or principles which operate naturally. A hypothesis implies the lack of enough evidence; therefore, it is merely a tentative explanation. A theory implies a much stronger accumulation of evidence. Therefore, it is stronger than a hypothesis, since it implies a greater probability of being truthful.

A law refers to a proposition which is well regulated in nature and which does not vary under a controlled set of conditions or events. These three states of formulary approach to a problem can be influx, and the addition of new evidence can shift the status and strength of each approach.

Just where the concept of psychoimmunology stands at present cannot be stated with accuracy, since it is relatively a new concept. A great deal of work is needed to classify its status properly. Hence the author has used the term theory rather loosely at this time in relation to psychoimmunology.

To hypothesize a belief or a certain formula, it is necessary to have some facts and then to treat them as if these were true. The investigator desires to discover the different relations between the facts he has derived from observation and those which he desires to uncover through further work with such clues as are available. His hypothesis need not necessarily be composed of observable facts, but the data certainly should have been gleaned from scientific observation. Hence, his deduced facts must be capable of standing scientific scrutiny. If these so-called facts are found wanting, then the hypothesis must be either changed or discarded after proper scientific investigation and the application of logic. If the results are not logical, they are faulty in some manner.

Theories have been often associated with speculation of an unverified nature. Moreover, these theories may be intimately associated with hypotheses, confirmed or not confirmed. Theories may even become scientific doctrines when derived from a group of testable propositions, and may hence gain recognition as scientific principles. Deductive theory evolves as an important tool for testing beliefs. Hence, epistomology evolves as the science of the method employed and the grounds for the knowledge thus obtained with reference to its limits and its validity (9).

The basis of theory is predicated on facts which come from observation. The tenets of such a theory are then open to test to determine the validity of the theoretical structure. The main reason for testing this structure or system is to be able to predict certain events and to understand the real *modus operandi* behind the theoretical structure, in order to determine the whys and wherefores. Hence, a theory consists of the explanation of facts derived from scientific observations.

As Wolman (10) so aptly wrote, various criteria are needed for credence in any scientific theory. He wrote about the necessity for "imminent truth." Thus, a scientific theory should not contain contradictions to the theory's main propositions. Furthermore, no contradictions should have arisen from experimental facts. Of exceptional importance is that scientific research must be based mainly upon the "discovery of truth."

Empirical events are employed to establish certain scientific laws. These separate events can be connected together so that reliable predictions can be formulated for presently unknown situations. This is common for the biologic and physical sciences. They contain empirical subject matter and are exemplified by anthropology, psychology, sociology, and economics, and they should certainly include the study of mankind and its place in the natural environment.

George Engel (11) commented that psychological phenomena should not have the terminology and the techniques of biochemistry applied to them. He argued for incorporating knowledge gleaned from such sciences to develop a comprehensive theory for psychology and behavior. However, he did not believe the problems of the "mind" would be solved by biochemical means alone. He did not think that psychologic science's development would become superfluous because of biochemical discoveries. He did stress that biologic knowledge was needed to further psychological knowledge.

Engel's approach is more oriented toward science than those of the strict Freudian, the neo-Freudian, or the more generalized psychodynamic schools. The construction of their theories is not usually founded upon a system used by pure science. The terminology they employ is certainly not used in the other sciences.

Bailey (12) wrote that Freud, at one phase of his career, tried to formulate an outline for scientific psychology which he termed "The Project," which was published. However, insufficient scientific data concerning neurophysiology caused Freud to abandon this approach. According to Bailey, this impasse forced Freud to begin his visionary psychologic speculations.

Concerning such psychologic speculations, Thigpen and Cleckley (13) called attention to many of the astonishing pronouncements made by Freud which were produced through mere assumption and analogy. As Bailey put it (14) "The supreme achievement of Sigmund Freud could be epitomized as his feat of inducing the world to accept his conclusions without permitting observation of his methods or rendering an account of his results." In the following paragraph Bailey wrote: "Psychoanalytic data are not reliable and repeatable, hence not scientific," and later on (p. 90) "Because of its method, psychoanalysis will forever remain bad science." Sidney Hook and others echoed a similar belief.

Webster (15) wrote about several types of analogies which are based upon the relationship of likenesses of one thing to another concerning the attributes, circumstances, or effects of each. Biologically speaking, an analogy is concerned with a correspondence in function between organs or parts of different function and origin. Logically, so wrote Webster, an analogy is a form of inference such that, if several things agree with each other in one or several respects, they will probably agree in still other ways.

Such a process is employed in almost every human endeavor, because any act whatsoever is usually compared with similar happenings. Even our common language habits contain analogous metaphors, in which one object or idea is employed in place of another by denoting a likeness between them, as with the use of a trope, simile, or comparison. In science we compare abnorms with norms. This has become routine.

The interpretation of data uses analogy in order to compare one's present results with those obtained previously by one or more observers, either by the same experimenter or by different persons. This really constitutes the basis for controlled studies. Hence, it appears unfounded to condemn any theory merely because it happens to argue through analogy. But this is not the important point. The crux of the matter lies in the source of the experiment or theory and whether or not it was performed according to accepted scientific procedures.

One investigator may produce a thoroughly logical set of scientific data. His procedure may have been rendered in the best of scientific tradition. Few will probably question his findings as to its veracity when these were attained from well controlled studies.

The trouble lies in their interpretation, which involves this pesky matter known as the analogical approach; for two well indoctrinated, well-trained scientists and even logicians, as a matter of fact, might arrive at two or more divergent views. Hence, it is the matter of interpreting scientific data which produces no little confusion.

Most if not all theories use analogy in formulating their own *modus operandi.* This is no indictment of good theory formation. However, such theories must have been founded on a scientific approach with the use of adequate controls; and, of equal importance, sound logic must have been employed to formulate both the theory and the results obtained from it.

There appears to be a ridiculous trend these days whenever students, residents, or graduate students wish to contribute their own beliefs while attacking or criticizing a theory. This takes the form of a game which is strongly reminiscent of the television game called "Jeopardy." In this TV program, all answers are given in the form of questions. With the students who discuss theoretical concepts also in the form of questions, one wonders why such a ritual is followed. Our only rationalization concerning this silly bit of decorum is that, by asking a question, one does not run the risk of differing with his learned teacher. Therefore, he does not incur the chance of receiving a poor grade.

Obviously, mature teachers and their students should avoid this ridiculous ceremonial by meeting whatever challenges are presented head on and by letting "the quips fall where they may"! In other words, a sound theory should be able to stand on its own two feet without ceremonials to protect it against injury. But, on the other hand, dissident teachers, who have little if any constructive worth in their arguments for or against theories, can be called by Professor Magidoff's term "superfluous men." Perhaps there are superfluous teachers and scientists. Arguments solely for the sake of further non-constructive ambiguous statements add little value to the understanding of a theory's functionings. As I wrote some time ago, "it is not a too difficult task to learn what others have written in our behalf. It is much harder to put our imagination and initiative to work at least to attempt to reward medical science for the wealth of information which others have given to us. We all tend to take too much for granted, and most of us as physicians are too critical of the work of others but not too productive so far as we ourselves are concerned." (16)

In an earlier paper (17), stress was placed on the brain sensitizations produced by one's environment. The sensitization-producing afferent stimuli are termed psychoimmunogens, which cause learning if one's neurologic pathways and input cortical centers function normally. Learning takes place because of the neurophysiochemical changes which are caused by the action of psychoimmunogens on the afferent neural receptors in the cerebral cortex.

Overlearning can be regarded as resulting from excessive psychoimmunogens which produce overstimulation of the brain's recording centers. In effect, such is a hypersensitization reaction. It follows that the realm between normal and abnormal learning processes is not abysmal.

Freudian *complexes* and also (Jungian and Adlerian) can be considered as being hypersensitive states of learning which resulted from the effects from overstimulation (overlearning). The psychoanalytic type of therapy reintroduces these stored (subconscious) results from learning as the analyst directs their reintroduction. This therapy resembles that employed by the allergist who produces immunity to allergens by very slowly introducing the offending allergen into the patient's body. In either case, too rapid introductions and or too strong doses of the offending agent may produce a surmenage of undesired reactions. With the allergist, his patient may exhibit a severe allergic reaction, while with the analyst a severe psychiatric reaction may ensue in the form of a severe depression or a suicidal attempt in his patient. Hence, both physicians must remain continually alert for such untoward reactions. As was mentioned previously, the Wier-Mitchell "rest cure" removes both types of patients from their irritating environments. The psychiatric patient is removed from further irritations from psychoimmunogens which produced his overlearning in the form of complexes; the allergic patient is removed from antigens which produced his form of allergic response, be it urticarial, an attack of asthma, or what not.

Along similar lines, the detection of psychologic complexes is discovered through the use of association tests which introduce key words (visual psychoimmunogens) which produce observable emotional reactions in a sensitized patient to related concepts. Similarly, the Rorschach test employs visual psychoimmunogens which can set off similar emotional reactions in a subject who has been previously sensitized to similar types of overlearning.

Sensory deprivations obviously decrease learning responses, while added combinations of sensory perceptions and their neural tracts bring added associated afferent neural stimuli to the recording centers of the brain. This is the basis for the Montessori teaching methods which use reinforcing psychoimmunogens to teach pupils, as with the aid of tactual stimuli, vision, and hearing. Perhaps the case of Alabama's Helen Keller is a case in point. She was without the use of vision and audition. Yet she was able to learn (sensitize the brain) merely with the use of her remaining afferent neural tracts which had to do with her touch and olfactory tracts (18).

Fuller (19) studied the behavior of dogs under various aspects of deprivation of sensory stimuli (environmental). He found that deprivation does not necessarily prevent normal development of intelligent behavior, but it interferes with behavior in vulnerable dogs. After isolation the perceptual stimuli were overwhelming. Also, genetic factors appeared to enter into the animals' reactions. Permanent retardation was a possibility. These findings appear to support the situation regarding Helen Keller's disabilities. So the lack of perception at birth in the human, who is devoid of all five afferent neural tracts, might well result in complete amentia.

Important as education is, if all students earned their doctorate degrees, who would remain to do the repair work? Learning and education are not the final answers for all of mankind's dilemmas. Perhaps it is fortunate that nature maintains its own checks and balances. The revered Milton summed it all when he wrote:

> Accuse not Nature;
> She hath done her part.
> Do thou but thine!

During my discussion with esteemed colleagues, many have expressed their decided interest in the Immunologic Theory. As a matter of fact, I have found it rather difficult to obtain serious arguments against this construct. However, some of these divergent points are presented for our readers so that they will become acquainted with some of the adverse arguments which have come to light.

The biggest hiatus arises whenever a humanist is confronted with a biologic concept which threatens his tenure of such subjects as soul and various religious tenets. Few humanists are trained by a biologic approach to behavior, particularly when applied to human beings. For them there remains the mysterious something which separates other animals from the human species. Brilliant scholars have argued over religious concepts probably since the inception of mankind. Far be it from me to attempt the interruption of their philosophic battles, for these might (or might not) contribute to the real understanding of behavior, human or otherwise.

One colleague pointed to my use of the word "volition" as a function of the will. That is correct. However, my explanation of volition is associated with the process of recall, as when the affect from an incoming psychoimmunogen becomes encoded in the cerebral cortex. If this is associated with a previously learned (encoded) cortical area, a surmenage of neuroelectrochemical energy is released, and this sets off what we conceive to be recall. We are just beginning to learn the many physiologic functions of the cerebral cortex. So volition can be regarded as the process of recall, that is, the releasing of stored data in the cerebral cortex. The Leyden Jar phenomenon does offer one explanation for this rather remarkable human ability.

Another colleague raised the point that only observable events in the neurons will determine the possibility of the allergic (immunologic) approach. My reply is agreeable to this point. Yet, allergists have not found specific antibodies for the physical allergies, although the latter certainly exists. We may not have all answers to various questions, but we are aware of the presence of such phenomena as the physical allergies.

The question was asked when I would agree that my theory will become disconfirmatory in principle. I presume this will happen when the theory is found not to be of value clinically or experimentally. This has not happened since its inception about forty years ago. Confirmatory data continues to aid the theory as time passes.

Another point raised against the theory consisted of a colleague being unable to imagine the brain reacting to allergic or immunologic stimuli when its main function is to process various intellectual data. I recall that nasal organ, which extrudes more or less from the human face, functions for ascertaining smell; yet, many times, excessive sneezing produced by certain irritating allergens can cause the affected person to forego the pleasures derived from enjoying perfume originating from various perfumed anatomic parts of the opposite sex.

One person asked if my theory, relating to hypersensitization, causes various forms of mental disease because of overlearning (hypersensitizations). I believe this is correct. Furthermore, most American and European schools of psychiatry follow this same approach.

The reader should continually remember that tissue sensitivity is an integral part of neural physiology. The fact that such tissue—and all living tissue, as a matter of fact—can become injured by noxious stimuli is a highly important point to retain. The living organism attempts to avoid pain, unless it suffers from some exotic disorder such as masochism. Pain is produced by frustratory happenings which occur often in one's daily life. If too painful events occur, certain defense mechanisms are available in the attempts to protect the individual from further harm. The individual fights or runs from his painful ecosystem. If he runs far enough, he breaks off from reality and thus becomes psychotic.

One colleague thought that more time should have been devoted to the various schools, such as the Freudian, the Neo-Freudian, and the various schools of behaviorism. I doubt if I could do justice to these theories within the confines of this relatively concise volume. I do not believe this is the time or the place for such consideration.

Another confrere asked what crucial test or experiment might disconfirm my thesis. I am answering this question by stating if we had enough expertise to find and identify the possibility of the presence or absence of psychoimmunogenic antibodies in the brain the answer would become crystal clear. I believe we would have the proper answer to this interesting question. Then the theory might become a law.

Another colleague wished to know if internal factors, such as an allergic response to one's own body chemistry, might be considered as an example of response to the theory. This subject has been studied extensively. Data on this topic will be found under the autoimmune diseases, of which more than a few are now known and can be found in most modern volumes of internal medicine and allergy. On this point, it might be highly worthwhile to give our students in psychology more scientific training rather than devoting so much time to mathematics.

If students of psychology would study many of the courses provided in the first two years of medicine, I am certain they would obtain knowledge which could not but help them materially to understand behavior and further assist them with their researches. Stress should be given to the studies which involve the neural sciences and immunology. Without such courses, students will continue to be devoid of highly important facts which they do not receive currently in many departments of psychology.

After all, the human brain and its functions are totally

dependent on the vital functionings of organs, glandular systems, and the other fundamental functioning body structures. How can an automobile function smoothly if one does not know how to set the carburetor so that it functions properly? Similarly, the brain cannot function properly if its working parts are faulty. All organs of the human, including the brain, are connected intimately with supporting systems. Trouble ensues when one or more do not work properly. The budding psychologist should be cognizant of this fact if he expects to contribute important knowledge to his field of endeavor.

Finally, every student should receive, as his first course in psychology, the all important study of learning, which serves as the foundation for an individual's present and future behavior. Furthermore, he should strive to update this subject as he advances with his psychologic studies. I hope fervently this volume has stressed adequately the prime importance of this one topic. I will consider my endeavors as successful if this one point forms an integral part of his adequate preparation for becoming a scholarly and scientific psychologist!

Postscript:
The Early Morning
Special

Rarely does an author divulge the circumstances which led him to write his tome. However, in this case, the reader might be interested in such facts. Besides, I have found it good practice to offer a pleasurable denouement for each course I teach at the university, for this allows the student better to understand the various circumstances which led to the writing of this book and the published articles which preceded its writing.

As has been stated previously, this theory was not born overnight. As a matter of fact, it took nearly 40 years to evolve its main points. Practically all the material came from the reading of the works of other investigators coupled with my beliefs which came to fruition as I engaged in the private practice of medicine and clinical research over the years. However, the real testing of the theory came about through the publication of many articles here and abroad as the theory evolved, with the clinical applications of this data.

Psychological theorizing is highly important; but, in my humble opinion, it should be based upon one's clinical findings, not alone from laboratory research, if it is to prove applicable to those many events which are met during one's lifetime. The theory must take cognizance of those important events which occur from the individual's inception, his birth, and the many pleasurable and painful events which are met during a lifetime. I doubt if the study of animal behavior, as observed by rabbits and rats in a maze or a box, can convey too much pertinent information of clinical import to the student of psychology. This study should be based upon behavior of the individual, which, in turn, is heavily dependent upon one's physiologic knowledge. After all, it is this basic procedure which makes all human wheels turn.

"The Early Morning Special," as my wife and I called this volume, arose through its writing which took place almost daily between two and six A.M. I soon discovered that the work could not be performed satisfactorily at other times due to the many pressures which are encountered with a busy daily psychiatric practice. However, during those wee hours of the morning, all is quiet and peaceful with the exception of my German shepherd, who insisted upon my study door being kept open so he could continue to watch over me.

As a matter of fact, I have used similar scheduling with my other writings and research during such small morning hours. But danger can arise from dropping a volume on the floor, an act that might awaken my family members prematurely.

I have been able to function adequately so far as my medical practice is concerned with these short hours for sleep. One merely has to get used to such a routine, though it may not prove satisfactory for others to follow. But if one wishes to accomplish as much as is humanly possible within a 24-hour span, the old saying of "early to bed and early to arise" will allow any diligent writer to turn out his own "early morning special" if his effort is tempered with a modicum of necessary restraint whenever and wherever indicated.

I hope that others will press the continuation of the present studies contained in this current "early morning special." The fields of psychology and psychiatry are badly in need of important further data which might well result from original cerebrations.

Glossary

Allergy   An abnormal state of hypersensitivity caused by exposure to certain allergens. Re-exposure may cause an altered capacity of the body to react normally.

Ambivalence   Existence of opposite feelings or attitudes towards a particular object, such as love and hate occurring simultaneously.

Amygdala   An almond-shaped structure below the hypothalamus.

Anamnestic response   The so-called "memory" response which takes place when pre-existing antibodies, which had disappeared from the blood, are formed again by a non-specific antigen. In other words, the cells of the body recall the initial response to an antigen and then reform these same antibodies.

Anaphylaxis   The sensitization of an individual to a protein or toxic substance rendering the individual vulnerable to a subsequent injection.

Anatomy   The study of the structure of animals and humans.

Anterior   In front of or the forward position of an object, such as an organ or skull.

Antibody   A protective substance created in the body as the result from the introduction of an antigen. Antibodies are types of serum globulius manufactured in lymphoid tissue.

Antigen   A material of high molecular weight, and composed of protein-like material, which is capable of stimulating the production of antibodies when introduced in the body of an animal or human.

Antigen competition   The introduction of more than one antigen concurrently can produce competition between the antigens with usually the stronger prevailing.

Antigens of self   The same as auto-immune bodies.

Auditory   Pertaining to hearing and the ears. The eighth cranial nerve (auditory) supplies the individual with such a means.

Autofrustration   Frustration produced by the individual and not because of the act of others (heterofrustration).

Autogenous   Originating within one's own body in contrast to heterogenous (originating outside one's body).

Autoimmune bodies   Immune bodies produced by one's own tissues thereby causing altered immunologic responses which are capable of producing certain diseases.

Autonomic   Functionally independent of self-controlling, as applied to the autonomic nervous system.

Autonomic nervous system   Is concerned mainly with maintaining the body's homeostasis.

Basal ganglia (basal nuclei)   Masses of gray matter centrally imbedded in the thalamus, comprising the corpus striatum, caudate and lenticuloform nuclei, amygdaloid, and claustum.

Behavior   The study of how one conducts himself, how he behaves or deports himself, or how a tissue or organ reacts to a stimulus.

Behaviorist   A psychologist who advocates behaviorism, a particular school in psychology which is interested, among other things, in the modification of behavior.

Betz cells of the brain   Portions of the motor cortex, in the cerebrum, which lead to the pyramidal systems.

Biology   The study of life processes and how organisms act during their life cycles.

Caesarian (Caesarian Section)   The delivery of an infant, usually at term, through an incision in the mother's uterus.

Caudate nucleus   Long horseshoe-shaped mass of gray matter which forms a portion of the corpus striatum and is closely related to the lateral ventricle throughout its entire extent.

Cerebral capacities   Involve orientation, memory, and intellectual functions, such as comprehension, problem solving, calculations, knowledge and, in summary, cerebration.

Cerebral hemispheres   One of the pair of structures constituting the largest portion of the brain. It is made up of the extensive cerebral cortex, corpus striatum, and rhinocephalon, and contains the third ventricle.

Cerebral imprinting   The receipt and the subsequent storage of afferent data received from one's environment which produces certain neuroelectrochemical changes in brain cells. This is closely related to learning.

Cerebration   The process of cerebrating, which is concerned with neural input into the brain, the neuroelectrochemical changes which ensue, their storage and recall (remembering).

Cervical os   The cervical opening at the outlet of the uterus.

Cholinergic   Producing acetycholine.

Cholinoceptive mechanism   A structure or organ which is receptive to actylcholinic agents.

Cinguate gypus   The arch-shaped convulsion at the top of the corpus callosum. The cellosal sulcus separates it from the corpus callosum.

C.N.S.   Abbreviation for central nervous system.

Commissures (cerebral)   Nerve fibers, including corpus callosum, which relay impulses from one cerebral cortex to the other.

Complexes   Term for a series of emotionally accentuated ideas in a repressed state (Brill).

Conditioning   A means for modifying an individual's behavior.

Consciousness   The state of being aware of one's sensory input to the cerebral cortex from one's environment.

Corpus callosum   An arched mass of white matter at the bottom of the longitudinal fissure, made up of transverse fibers which connect the two cerebral hemispheres.

Cortico-spinal tracts   Portions from the pyramidal nerve tracts from the brain and forming the lateral, medial an anterior branches.

Crede   Dropping solution of silver nitrate in newborn child's eyes to prevent possible blindness due to gonorrheal infection.

Cytoplasm   The protoplasm of a cell not including the nucleus.

Decortate animal   An animal with its brain removed.

Decussion   The crossing of neural tracts from one side of the brain or spinal cord to the other side.

Dendrite   A tree-shaped or branched protoplasmic process from a nerve cell which has the ability to conduct nerve impulses to the body of the nerve cell.

Depression   Emotional dejection with absence of hope or cheerfulness.

Ecologist   A person who is interested in and studies the environment.

EEG - electroencephalogram   A graphic record obtained by the recording of electric currents produced in the brain via electrodes applied to the scalp, to the surface of the brain itself or placed within the brain substance.

Electrical potentials (in the brain and central nervous system)   Amounts or changes in the degree of electrical currents which pass between two different electrodes placed in various positions as on the individual's scalp, as employed with the electroencephalograph.

Electrode   A device employed between an electrical conductor and the object to which electric current is to be supplied.

Electrokinetic phenomena   Refers to motion caused by the flow of electric current.

Electroshock (E.C.T.)   Electric shock produced by placing electrodes usually to the opposite sides of one's head for the treatment mainly of depressive disorders.

Emotions   States of mental excitement or dejection characterized by such changes in one's feelings or affect.

Encoding   Recording of afferent stimuli in the brain cells which are affected by neuroelectrochemical changes thus produced.

Endocrine   Refers to glandular types of bodily reactions.

Energy gradients   Refers to various stimuli which are perceived by an individual. These gradients vary in intensity, depending upon the degree of energy employed in producing such stimuli.

Engram   The permanent trace left by a stimulus in the protoplasm of tissue. In psychology, it is a latent memory picture.

Environment   The sum total of all the elements, conditions, and objects which surround an individual.

Eosinophilia   Those blood cells which stain with eosin (red color) and accumulate in large amounts in the blood as is the case with allergies.

Epistemology   The theory or the science of the method or methods used for knowledge, especially their limits and their validity.

Estrouscycle   Relates to the menstrual cycle (see ovulation).

Exteroceptive stimuli   Perceptual stimuli which are carried via the five afferent tracts to the brain.

Exteroceptors   Sensory nerve terminals which can be stimulated by the immediate external environment, such as those nerve terminals in the mucous membranes and skin.

Extrapyramidal pathways (system)   In contrast to the more direct pyramidal pathway, the extrapyramidal system reach segemental levels of distribution after many detours with neuronal chains synaptically interrupted in basal ganglia, subcortical ganglia, and the reticular areas. Extrapyramidal functions consist of helping associated movements, as swinging the arms while walking, postural adjustments, and autonomic integration. It is difficult to separate it from the pyramidal pathways.

Fascicles   A cluster or small bundle of nerve or muscle fibers.

Fetus   The developing young in human uterus after the second month of gestation.

Fontanelle   A membrane-covered soft spot in an incompletely ossified skull bone.

Fractionates   Separate constituents of a liquid substance.

Freudian   Pertaining to the doctrines of Sigmund Freud about mental disorders or abnormal behavior, based upon the operations of unconscious sexual repressions in patient.

Frustrant   The individual or that part of the individual which is being frustrated (not allowed to act).

Frustration   The inability to achieve a particular goal because of a force, external or internal, which interferes with one's desires. This force is called the frustrator.

Frustrator   A person or agent which causes frustration.

Genes   Biologic units of heredity in particular sections of a particular chromosome.

Genitourinary   Refers to origin within the genital and urinary portions of the body.

Gestalt   A school of psychology which claims that those objects of which one is conscious arrive as complete and unanalyzable forms or wholes within the brain. These objects cannot be split into smaller portions.

Gestation   The development of the young in viviparous animals from the time of the ovum's fertilization.

Globus pallidus   A smaller and more median portion of the lenticuloform nucleus that is separated from the putamen by the external medullary lamina and divided by it into the internal and external portions.

Gum ball machine   Like I said, Man, y'know, like getting gum from it, man, and popping it in your mouth. Man, chew and crack it like hell, y'know, and like I said, man, drive the other cats nuts, man, y'know, like I said! Dig it?

Hapten (or *haptene*)   Often is a polysaccharide, in naturally occurring antigens, which can produce an antibody. Arsenilic acid derivatives appear to have the same capability.

Hemophobia   The fear caused by seeing blood.

Heredity   The transmission, by genes, of particular traits which are located in the gene's autosome.

Heterofrustration   Frustration produced by others rather than by the individual, which is autofrustration.

Heterogenous   Not originating within one's body, of outside origin.

Hippocampus   This forms the larger portion of the olfactory cerebral cortex. It is called Ammon's norm because its curved shape forms the medial part of the lateral ventricle's floor.

Histamine   A chemical substance, called an amine, which is found in all living tissues. It dilates capillary blood vessels and stimulate secretion in the stomach. If given in tiny doses which are slowly increased, it is employed to desensitize tissues.

Histic   Usually refers to a response from a tissue or organ in contrast to a *nousic* response which refers to the process of cerebration (thinking).

Homeostasis   The tendency of an individual to return to a state resembling normalcy, stability, or uniformity.

Hormone   A material, produced by the body, mostly by the endocrine glands.

Hypertrophy   The morbid overgrowth of a tissue or organ because of an increase of its constituent cells.

Hypothalamus   A portion of the diencephalon forming the floor and portion of the lateral wall of the third ventricle. It includes the optic chiasma, mamillary bodies, tuber cinereum, infundibulum and the hypothesis. These govern visceral activities, water balance, temperature, sleep, et cetera.

Immunity   Acquired security against a particular poison or disease or substance. The condition of becoming or being immune from certain noxious substances, various poisons, or certain diseases or substances.

Immunoelectrophoresis   An electrical method for separating antigen from antibody.

Immunology   The portion of biology which is interested in the study of immunity.

Inhibition (neural)   Restraint or arrest of neural impulses.

Integument   Another name for the skin.

Interceptive neural stimuli   Originate within one's brain, possibly because of the discharge of brain potentials which result from learning procedures.

Internal capsule   A whitish body, containing nerve fibers, which connect one cerebral hemisphere with the other. It lies above the thalamus.

Ionic fluxes   Pertains to movements of ions or atoms carrying a positive charge (caton) or a negative charge (anion). The ionic theory that molecules, going into solution, break up into positive and negative ions. The positive ions go to the negative pole, while the negative ones migrate to the positive pole on passage of an electric current.

Lacrimation   Watering of the eyes.

Latent period   Another name for stimulus trace where a stimulus does not immediately produce a response.

Lewis' triple response (of skin)   The injection of a tiny amount of histamine or an antigen produces swelling, redness, and itching in the area of skin which has been so treated.

Leyden jar   An apparatus which is capable of storing electricity (electric potentials).

Library theory   A concept whereby those changes resulting from learning are stored in one's cerebral archives for future reference similar to data which is kept in a library.

Limbic system (visceral brain)   Designates the limbic lobe and the infolded hippocampus, the amygdala, septal nuclei, hypothalamus, anterior thalamic nuclei, portions of the blood ganglia, and possibly the epithalamus. The term limbic system is used interchangeably with rage, fear, sexual behavior, and motivation.

Lower motor nueron lesion   Interruption of nerve impulses produced by a defect in the lower portion of the nervous system.

Marshall-white syndrome   A skin disorder or conflict produced by a disruption between skin constricting and dilutive factors, caused by long term emotional upset.

Masochism   Abnormal sexual pleasure derived from the receipt of pain-producing stimuli, usually effected by sadists on willing subjects.

Maturation   Arriving at one's full development - growing up.

Medulla (oblongata)   A body, containing nerve tracts, which lies above the pons and connects with the spinal cord. It lies above the fourth ventricle and is ventral to the cerebellum.

Memory response   Recalling some learned data, possibly through the action of the Leyden jar discharge type of phenomena. Very similar to an anamnestic response.

Mind-body concept (psycho-soma)   A possibly false belief that disorders of the mind and body are different in origin.

Mitochrondria   Rod-shaped structures or small granules in cell cytoplasm found with differential staining.

Montessori method   Named after Dr. Marie Montessori, of Italy, who employed the sense of touch to help acquaint her pupils with other learning procedures as with hearing and seeing. The sense of touch is also employed with Braille, allowing the blind to read.

Motivation   The state of being impelled or being supplied with a motive or incentive. The desire for attaining a particular goal.

Motor   Nerve, nerve center, or muscle which produces movement.

Molecular approach   Accumulation of scientific facts from the molecular structures and their functions.

Myelinated fibers   Fibers which are surrounded by a grayish-white covering called the white substance of Schwann.

Neocortex (neopallium)   The newer portion of the cerebral cortex which is located near the skull. The pallium contains a distinctive layer of cellular elements.

Neo-Freudian   A newer school of Freudianism whose main purpose is to shorten psychoanalytic techniques which otherwise could last for years.

Neonate   Newly born infant.

Neural sciences - neurosciences   Studies in such nerve-related subjects as neuroanatomy, neurophysiology, neuropathology and immunology. The main purpose is to discover how learning takes place.

Neurodermatoses   Various skin disorders thought to be produced by emotional tensions.

Neuroleptic drugs   Medications which can produce symptoms resembling certain disorders of the nervous system.

Nissl bodies   These are large granular protein bodies staining with basic dyes and forming the reticulum of the cytoplasm in nerve cells. These nissl bodies contain ribonucleoprotein as a main constituent.

Nousic   A type of cerebral response involving cerebration, such as sensory input in the cortex, its storage and retrieval (recall).

Olfactory nerve   The cranial nerve employed for the sensation connected with smell.

Ontology   The complete developmental history of the individual organism.

Operant conditioning   Are instrumental conditioning procedures.

Optic   Pertaining to the eyes and sight. The optic nerve supplies this for the individual.

Optic chiasma   The crossing or decussation of the optic nerve fibers from the medial half of the retina on the ventral (bottom) surface of the brain.

Optic tracts   Those nerve tracts, of the optic nerves, which supply sight.

Organ of Corti   The spiral organ which receives nerve fibers for hearing and sends out central neural branches to the dorsal and ventral cochlear nuclei.

Overlearning (Hull)   Excessive learning comparable to a state of hypersensitivity to particular stimuli which act upon the cortical cells to cause excessive neuroelectrochemical changes.

Ovulation   The discharge of an unimpregnated and mature ovum from the ovary.

Papez-MacLean pathways   Nerve tracts connecting the basal ganglia with the cerebral cortex. These neural pathways convey impulses to and from such structures.

Parasympathetic (craniosacral)   A part of the autonomic

nervous system.

Pathophysiology   The study of abnormal physiologic phenomena.

Pavlovian scratch reflex   Scratching the back or belly of an animal causes it to use his leg as though it were scratching the source of the stimuli. This is usually a pleasure producing stimulus for the affected animal.

Perception   The conscious mental registration of a sensory stimulus.

Perceptive neural tracts   These are associated with afferent stimuli from one's environment which acquaint the individual's central nervous system via seeing, hearing, smelling, tasting, and touch.

Phenothiazines   A family of medications employed for treating certain nervous and mental disorders.

Physical allergies   Allergic reactions produced by heat, cold, and pressure in a sensitive person.

Physiology   The study of bodily functions.

Pituitary hormone   A hormone derived from the pituitary gland.

Polygraphic tracings   Equipment for simultaneously recording mechanical or electrical impulses set up by respiratory movements, pulse waves, blood pressure changes, and the psychogalvanic reflex.

Pons   A body of nervous tissue which is a part of the central nervous system. It lies between the medulla oblongata and the cerebellum. It consists of a pars dorsalis and pars basalaris.

Prauschnitz-Kustner antibodies   A particular type of serum globulin produced by a specific antigen and demonstrating a specific reaction.

Prenate   The fetus prior to birth.

Primates   Advanced members of the ape family which stand erect, such as gorillas and even mankind.

Posterior   The back portion of an object.

Psyche   Refers to "mind" reactions, such as cerebration.

Psychiatry   The study of abnormal behavior, usually applied to humans. It is also defined as the study of diseases of the "Mind" or intellect.

Psychallergen, psychoimmunologen, psychoantigen   These terms are used interchangeably in this book. They denote afferent impulses which enter neural brain cells to cause neuroelectrochemical changes therein to produce cerebral encoding (learning).

Psychoallergy (in Dorland's Medical Dictionary, 24th Ed., p. 1243)   A condition of sensitization to certain words, ideas, people and other symbols of emotional patterns. (I never could have manufactured such a capable definition for this term.)

Psychoanalysis   A Freudian technic whereby the patient, lying on a couch, reports every thought which comes to his mind through free association. Thus, complexes are discovered and slowly treated.

Psychogalvanic readings   Those recordings of electrical changes which are produced by emotional stress.

Psychoimmunology   The author's theory involving studies with behavior which are related closely to findings from immunology.

Psychology   The study of behavior. It can be regarded as an offshoot of biology.

Psychopathology   A branch of medicine or psychology which deals with mental and emotional dysfunctions.

Psychophysiological diseases (psychosomatic)   Bodily and emotional disorders produced by overactions of the autonomic nervous system.

Psychosurgery   A surgical technic which attacks various brain nuclei and nerve tracts.

Psychotropic drugs   Those medications or substances which exert their effects on one's cerebration.

Putamen   The lateral medullary lamina separates the putamen from globus pallidus. The putamen is the larger portion of the lentiform nucleus.

Pyramidal pathways (tracts)   Includes portions of the extrapyramidal tract and is composed mainly by the corticospinal tract (See extrapyramidal system.)

Pyriform area   The lateral exposed part of the olfactory cerebral cortex in lower animals.

Reflex   The involuntary movement of an object or part of it to a stimulus.

Refractory state   A state where nothing appears to happen following the introduction of an antigen or a psychoantigen, prior to the formation of antibody or a state of hypersensitivity from a psychoantigen.

Reticular network   Pertaining to or resembling a network, especially a network of structures dispersed around the medullary brain stem.

Retina   The innermost of the eyeball's three layers. It surrounds the vitreous humor and continues posteriorly with one optic nerve. The retina contains an outer pigmented layer and an inner transparent layer.

Rorschach test   A psychologic test which employs ink splotches. Patients view the series of spots which produce certain associations they have formed from the effects of previous sensory stimuli on the brain cells.

Sadism   Abnormal sexual pleasure derived from painful experiences produced by others.

Scarify   To scratch the intact skin so that certain allergic substances can be rubbed into these areas to determine if sensitivity to each may exist.

Schizophrenia   A particular form of mental disorder. Its name is derived from splitting of the personality in the involved individual.

Security blanket   The blanket used in early childhood, which the child cherishes to the point where he resents being separated from his pet blanket.

Sense of taste   Involves 5th, 7th and 9th cranial nerves.

Sensitivity   Denoting a response to a stimulus in an acute and rapid manner. Neural tissues are characterized by their states of sensitivity.

Sensoria   Pertaining to one's sensory nerves, especially their terminations in the brain.

Sensory deprivations   Being without the use of seeing, hearing, smelling, tasting, or feeling, producing inability to learn.

Sensory intake   This is related to encoding of the brain cells from afferent neural stimuli stimulated by environmental energies.

Set   Other terms are purpose, insight, attention, attitude, need, vector, preoccupation, perservation, expectancy, hypothesis, and stimulus trace (Hull). It is produced by at least a previous sensitization which produces memory. The individual who shows a "set" appears unable to react to a specific stimulus until some time has passed. It is closely related to the refractory state in immunology.

Skinner box   A box, devised by Professor B. F. Skinner, in which various mazes and conditioning procedures are carried forth for experiments in psychology.

Sociology   The study which deals with social relations and their various disorders.

Soma   Refers to bodily reactions such as heart disease, headaches, et cetera.

Stimulation   The process of stimulating as by the action of a nerve impulse upon its receptor.

Stimulus   Any agent which produces a functional or trophic reaction in irritable tissue or a receptor.

Stimulus trace   A certain state in the brain caused by a stimulus. This pehnomenon is related to "set" where a lag in action occurs before the individual reacts to the stimulus.

Surmenage   A sudden outpouring similar to a break in a dam causing a sudden surge of water to gush forth.

Synapse   The location when a nerve impulse is transmitted from one neuron to another. This is also known as the synaptic junction.

Syncope   Unconsciousness of usually short duration as produced by fainting.

Tactile stimuli   Stimuli associated with the sensation of touch.

Target organ   An area or organ upon which nerve impulses (usually autonomic in origin) act. In psychophysiologic disorders, weaker organs, because of faulty heredity, may become target organs.

Thalamus   The larger and the middle part of the diencephalon which forms the lateral wall to the 3rd ventricle. It lies between the hypothalamus and the epithalamus. It is the main relay center for sensory impulses to the brain cortex.

Therapist   One who treats people with disorders.

Thermocouple   A scientific device for measuring small variations in temperature.

Thinking   A more acceptable term would be cerebration which involves receipt of sensory impulses, their storage, and their subsequent recall.

Thoracolumbar (sympathetic)   Components of the sympathetic nervous system.

Threshold   The particular point where a specific stimulus produces a sensation which can be recognized by the subject.

Trans 2 methyl   2 hexenoic acid, a peculiar, pungent odorous substance found in the sweat of certain psychotic patients.

Transplants   Foreign tissues or organs used in place of the original structures. However, tissues from the same individual may be grafted for such a purpose (autotransplant).

Trauma   Injury or a wound. Birth trauma is the shock experienced by the newly born infant while being born.

Trophic   Pertaining to nutrition.

Tropic   Tending to turn towards or change, as a leaf turning towards a light source.

Uncinate brain area   The area of the brain which lies in the postero-lateral area and which receives visual stimuli.

Upper motor neuron lesion   Interruption of nerve impulses produced by some defect in the upper part of the nervous system.

Uterus   A hollow muscular organ in females which shields the embryo (and fetus) while it maturates.

Vasoconstriction   Narrowing action on blood vessels through its nerve supply.

Vibruncules   Term employed by Doctors Hartley, Priestley, and others denoting infinitesimal nerve vibrations to the brain which were believed to produce learning.

Visual receptors   The rods and cones of the retina.

Word association tests   Using a list of words read or heard by the patient, certain key words produce emotional reactions which are observed and recorded by various methods.

Word blindness   Inability to recognize written words as symbols of ideas. Alexia (dyslexia) a word blindness is the inability to read because of a disorder of Brodman's cortical areas 18 and 19.

References

Chapter 1

1. Marshall, Wallace (21 July 1937). "Suggestions for studies in psychology and psychiatry." *Medical Record* 146: 71-73.
2. ———. (July 1936). "The mechanisms of psychoallergy." *American Journal of Psychiatry,* 76-85.
3. ———. (1940). "The immunological concept of learning." *Journal of General Psychology* 22:193-98. (This paper was received by the journal editor on 27 September 1938.)
4. ———. (1939). "Psychiatric evaluation of afferent stimuli and learning processes." *Psychiatric Quarterly* 13:332.
5. ———. (1939). "Psychoallergy in general practice." *Clinical Medicine and Surgery* 44:149.
6. ———. (1938). "Pathologic physiology and the psychoneuroses." *Northwest Medicine* 37:5.
7. ———. (March 1941). "Comments on personality, unconditioning and frustration." *Medical Times* 69:106.
8. ———. (March 1938). "Comparative study of etiological factors in allergic and psychopathological conditions." *Virginia Medical Monthly.*
9. Priestley, Joseph (1775). *Hartley's Theory of the Human Mind, on the Principles of the Association of Ideas with Essays Relating to the Subject of It.* Printed by J. Johnson, No. 72, St. Paul's Church Yard, London.

Chapter 2

1. Marshall, Wallace (January 1970). "Immunologic psychology and psychiatry." *Journal of The Medical Association of The State of Alabama* 39:649-57.
2. ———. (September 1969). "Immunologic augmentations per learning and psychiatry."

3. Marshall, Wallace and J. S. Tarwater (March 1938). "Comparative study of etiologic factors in allergic and psychopathologic conditions." *Virginia Medical Monthly* 65: 154-62.

4. Jegorow, B. (15 May 1936). "The laws of allergy." *Weiner Klinische Wochenschrift,* 49-623.

5. Sheldon, J. W., R. G. Lovell and K. P. Matthews (1967). *A Manual of Clinical Allergy.* W. B. Saunders Co., Philadelphia.

6. Weiser, R. S., Q. N. Myrvick and N. N. Perasall (1969). *Fundamentals of Immunology.* Leas and Febiger, Phildelphia.

7. Nelson, W. E. (1964) *Textbook of Pediatrics.* W. B. Saunders Co., Philadelphia, 8th ed., p. 25.

8. Marshall, Wallace (July 1936). "Psychopathology and treatment of the Parkinsonian syndrome and other postencephaletic sequelae." *Journal of Nervous and Mental Disease* 84:27.

9. ——— and V. F. Marshall (May 1937). "Traumatism and Parkinsonismus." *Journal of the Medical Association of The State of Alabama* 6:358-62.

10. Marshall, Wallace (March 1940). "Psychologic observations with reeducation in a case of multiple sclerosis." *Archives of Physical Therapy* 21:164.

11. Case from author's files.

12. Heath, R. G. (May 1967). "Schizophrenia: pathogenetic theories." *International Journal of Psychiatry* 3:407-10.

13. *Neurosciences Research Program Bulletin,* 31 December 1967, p. 10.

14. Schmitt, F. O. (1967). "Molecular parameters in brain function," in the Nobel Conferences *The Human Mind,* North-Holland. (Organized by Gustavus Adolphus College, St. Peter, Minnesota.)

15. Wolpe, J. (1965). *Psychotherapy by Reciprocal Inhibition.* Stanford University Press, Palo Alto, Calif.

16. Hebb, D. O. (1943). *Organization of Behavior: A Neuropsychological Theory.* John Wiley and Sons, Inc., N. Y. (First Science ed. printing, 1961).

17. Lewis, T. (1927). *The Blood Vessels of the Human Skin and*

their Responses. Shaw and Sons, Ltd., London.

18. Sherman, W. B. (1968). *Hypersensitivity, Mechanisms and Management.* W. B. Saunders Co., Philadelphia, 86-91.

19. Criep, L. H. (1969). *Clinical Immunology and Allergy.* Greene and Stratton, N. Y., 427-42.

20. Rapaport, H. B. and S. M. Linde (1970). *The Complete Allergy Guide.* Simon and Schuster, N. Y., 325-30.

21. Sheldon, J. M., R. G. Lovell and K. P. Matthews (1967). *A Manual of Clinical Allergy.* W. B. Saunders and Co., Philadelphia, 143, 299.

22. Stein, M. and R. Schiavi (1967). In Freedman and Kaplan's *Comprehensive Textbook of Psychiatry.* Williams and Wilkins Co., Baltimore, 1,069-70.

23. Engels, W. D. and E. D. Wittkower. In Freedman and Kaplan's *Comprehensive Textbook of Psychiatry,* 1,097.

Chapter 3

1. Milner, P. M. (1970). *Physiological Psychology.* Holt, Rinehart and Winston, Inc., N. Y.

2. Krech, D., R. S. Crutchfield and N. Livson (1969). *Elements of Psychology.* Alfred A. Knopf, N. Y., 73-87.

3. Hebb, D. O. (1966). *A Textbook of Psychology.* W. B. Saunders Co., Philadelphia, 2nd ed.

4. Gardner, E. (1968). *Fundamentals of Neurology.* W. B. Saunders Co., Philadelphia, 5th ed.

5. Krech, D. et al. *Elements of Psychology,* 468-69.

Chapter 4

1. Marshall, Wallace (June 1970). "The psychology of being hurt." *Journal of the Louisiana State Medical Society* 122:180-84.

2. Dubois, R. (1968). *So Human an Animal.* Scribner, N. Y., 89.

3. Marshall, Wallace (July 1969). "Normal and abnormal behavior from learning." *Journal of The Medical Association State of Alabama* 39:40.

4. Odom, E. P. (1963). *Ecology.* Holt, Rinehart and Winston,

N. Y., 3.

5. Marshall, Wallace (June 1971). "Biologic factors in Ethology." *Journal of The Medical Association of The State of Alabama* 40:800-04.

Chapter 5

1. Hilgard, E. R. (1956). *Theories of Learning*. Appleton-Century-Crofts, Inc., N. Y., 2nd ed., 1.
2. Humphrey, G. and R. V. Coxon (1963). *The Chemistry of Thinking*. Charles C. Thomas, Springfield, 112.
3. Morgan, C. T. (1956). *Introduction to Psychology*. McGraw-Hill, N. Y., 107.
4. Ruch, F. (1958). *Psychology and Life*. Scott, Foresman and Co., Chicago, 5th ed., 297.
5. Leyden Jar in *Encyclopaedia Britannica*. Wm. Benton, Chicago, (1959), vol. 12, 989.
6. Nousic is the term coined by one of us (W.M.), circa 1937. The word originates from the Greek "nouos" meaning mind. The term refers to the affecting of cerebration or the intellectual process in contradistinction to the word "histic" which refers to a tissue, organ, or cellular manifestation. For example, a histic reaction takes place when an individual breathes, raises an arm, or whistles. A nousic type of reaction occurs when one thinks or reasons. The term "nousic" is in *Dorland's Illustrated Medical Dictionary*. W. B. Saunders Co., Philadelphia, 24th ed., 1965, 1,023.
7. Hebb, D. O. (1943). *Organization of Behavior: A Neuropsychological Theory*. John Wiley and Sons, Inc. (First Science ed. printing 1961), Introduction, xi.
8. Ibid., xiii.
9. Ibid., xvi.
10. Ibid., xix.
11. Ibid., 2.
12. Ibid., 5.
13. Ibid., 6.
14. Ibid., 128.
15. Hull, C. L. (1943). *Principles of Behavior: An Introduction*

to *Behavior Theory.* Appleton-Century, N. Y.

16. Ibid., 11.
17. Ibid., 12.
18. Ibid., 13.
19. Ibid., 127.
20. Kohler, W. (1947). *Gestalt Psychology.* New American Library (Mentor Book), N. Y., 7th printing, 33.
21. Ruch, F. L. (1958). *Psychology and Life.* Scott, Foresman and Co., Chicago, 5th ed., 297.
22. Ibid., 300-01.
23. Kimble, G. A. (1956). *Principles of General Psychology.* Ronald Press Co., N. Y., 215.
24. Ibid., 215.
25. Morgan, C. T. (1956). *Introduction to Psychology.* McGraw-Hill, N. Y., 127.
26. Ibid., 11.
27. Hilgard, E. R. (1956). *Theories of Learning.* Appleton-Century-Crofts, Inc., N. Y., 5.
28. Ibid., 7, 8.
29. Ibid., 9.
30. John, E. R. (1967). In Freedman and Kaplan's *Comprehensive Textbook of Psychiatry.* Williams and Wilkins Co., Baltimore, 150-51
31. Humphrey, G. and R. V. Coxon (1963). *The Chemistry of Thinking.* Charles C. Thomas, Springfield.
32. Mitchell, S. R., J. M. Beaton and R. J. Bradley. "Biochemical transfer of acquired information." *International Revue of Neurobiology.* In press.
33. Smithies, J. R. (1971). *Brain Mechanisms and Behavior.* Blackwell, Oxford, England.

Chapter 6

1. Powers, W. T. (26 January 1973). "Feedback: beyond behaviorism." *Science* 179:351-56.
2. Stevens, S. S. (4 December 1970). "Neural events and psychophysical law." *Science* 170:1,043-50.
3. Bryant, Rodney C. et al. (3 November 1972). "Nonspecific behavioral effects of substances from mammalian brain."

Science 178:521-23.

4. Ingle, David J. and Gerald E. Schneider (19 June 1970). "Brain mechanisms and vision: subcortical systems." *Science* 168:1,493-94.

5. Paolino, Ronald M. and H. M. Levy (14 May 1971). "Lateral hypothalamus: reevaluation of function in motivated feeding behavior." *Science* 172:744-46.

6. Smith, Douglas E. et al. (6 February 1970). "Lateral hypothalamic control of killing: evidence for a cholinoceptic mechanism." *Science* 167:900-01.

7. DeLong, M. R. (23 March 1973). "Putamen: activity of single units during slow and rapid arm movements." *Science* 179:1,240-42.

8. Yen, S. S. C. (1973). "Hypothalamic-pituitary discharge." *Reproductive Endocrinology.* (Medcom.) Wyeth Laboratories, Philadelphia, 15.

Chapter 7

1. Gardner, E. (1968). *Fundamentals of Neurology.* W. B. Saunders Co., Philadelphia, 172-73.

2. Wechsler, L. S. (1963). *Clinical Neurology.* W. B. Saunders Co., Philadelphia.

3. Alpers, B. J. (1963). *Clinical Neurology.* F. A. Davis Co., Philadelphia.

4. Chusid, J. G. and J. J. McDonald (1964). "Correlative neuroanatomy and functional neurology." *Lange Medical Publications.* Los Altos, California, 12th ed., 17.

Chapter 8

1. Comfort, Alexander (6 May 1972). "What is a doctor?" *The Lancet,* 973.

2. Milner, P. M. (1970). *Physiological Psychology.* Holt, Rinehart and Winston, Inc., N. Y., 39.

3. Krech, et al. *Elements of Psychology,* 577.

4. Chusid and McDonald. "Correlative neuroanatomy and functional neurology," 71, 148.

5. Akiskal, H. S. and W. T. McKinney (5 October 1973). "Depressive disorders: toward a unified hypothesis." *Science* 182, 20-28.

6. Noyes, A. P. and L. C. Kolb (1963). *Modern Clinical Psychiatry*. W. B. Saunders Co., Philadelphia, 6th ed., 384-414.

7. Dorfman, W. (1966). *Closing the Gap Between Medicine and Psychiatry*. Chas. C. Thomas, Springfield, 16.

8. Marshall, Wallace (1969). *Journal of The Medical Association of The State of Alabama* 38:622.

9. Doty, R. W. (1967). In Freedman, A. M. and H. L. Kaplan. *Comprehensive Textbook of Psychiatry*. Williams and Wilkins Co., Baltimore, 125-26.

10. Marshall, Wallace (June 1970). "The psychology of being hurt." *Journal of The Louisiana State Medical Society*.

11. Smith, K., G. F. Thompson and H. D. Koster (17 October 1969). "Sweat in schizophrenics: identification of odorous substance." *Science*, 398.

12. Noval, J. J. and T. S. S. Mao (April-May 1970). "An unidentified antigen present in abnormal amount in schizophrenia serum." *Behavioral Neuropsychiatry* 2:27.

13. Marshall, Wallace (1969). "Immunologic augmentations for learning and psychiatry." *Journal of The Medical Association of The State of Alabama* 29:243.

14. Travis, R. P. and D. Sparks (1967). "Unitary responses and discrimination learning in squirrel monkey: The globus, pallidus." *Psychology and Behavior*. The Pergamon Press, Great Britain 3:187-96.

15. Gardner. *Fundamentals of Neurology*, 242.

16. Lief, H. I., V. F. Lief and N. R. Lief (1963). *The Psychological Basis of Medical Practice*. Hoeber Medical Division of Harper and Row, N. Y., 49.

Chapter 9

1. Marshall, Wallace (January 1969). "Learning and the development of frustration." *Journal of The Medical Association of The State of Alabama* 38:622-26.

2. Silver, A. (1963). In *Dyslexia*, edited by A. H. and V. T. Kenney. C. V. Mosby Co., St. Louis, 81.

3. *Dorland's Illustrated Medical Dictionary* (1965). W. B. Saunders Co., Philadelphia, 24th ed., 588.

4. *Blakiston's New Gould Medical Dictionary* (1951). The

Blakiston Co., Philadelphia, 1st ed., 402.

5. Deese, J. and S. H. Hulse (1967). *The Psychology of Learning*. McGraw-Hill, Toronto, 3rd ed., 134.

6. Wolman, B. (1968). *Scientific Psychology*. Basic Books, Inc., N. Y., 14.

7. Hofling, C. K. (1963). *Textbook of Psychiatry for Medical Practice*. J. B. Lippincott Co., Philadelphia, 90.

8. Hebb, D. O. (1949). *The Organization of Behavior: A Neurophysiological Theory*. John Wiley and Sons, Inc., N. Y., 232.

9. Goldberg, H. K. (1963). In Kenney, A. H. and V. T. Kenney *Dyslexia, Diagnosis and Treatment of Reading Disorders*. C. V. Mosby Co., St. Louis, 92-93.

10. Marshall, W., C. J. White, and L. H. Kwong (May 1965). "Dermatologic and psychosomatic aspects of the Marshall-White Syndrome." *Cutis* 1.

11. Marshall, W. and C. J. White (1933). "Localized areas of ischemia on the hands." *Journal of Laboratory and Clinical Medicine* 18:386.

12. White, C. J., W. Marshall and L. H. Kwong (1965). "Marshall-White Syndrome: evidence of vasomotor conflict in a particularly severe case." *Journal of The Medical Association of The State of Alabama* 34:249.

Chapter 10

1. Evans, J. P. (December 1966). "Advances in the understanding and treatment of head injury." *Canadian Medical Association Journal* 95:1, 337-48.

2. Chusid and MacDonald. *Correlative Neuroanatomy and Functional Neurology,* 15.

3. MacLean, P. D. (1957). "Chemical and electrical stimulation of hippocampus in unrestrained animals." *American Medical Association Archives of Neurology and Psychiatry* 78:113-42.

Chapter 11

1. *Encyclopaedia Britannica.* Wm. Benton, Publisher, Chicago,

vol. 15, 1973, 896.
2. Marshall, Wallace (January 1970). "Immunologic psychol-
    ogy and psychiatry." *Journal of The Medical Association
    of The State of Alabama* 39:649-57.
3. Cecil-Loeb (1936). *Textbook of Medicine.* Beason, P. and
    W. McDermott (eds.). W. B. Saunders Co., Philadelphia,
    778-79.
4. Branch, C. H. H., H. B. Fowler and S. W. Grant (1972). *Psy-
    choneurotic Depression/Anxiety.* Pfizer Laboratories,
    N. Y.

Chapter 12

1. Marshall, Wallace (June 1970). "The psychology of being
    hurt." *Journal of The Louisiana State Medical Society*
    122:180-84.
2. Gardner. *Fundamentals of Neurology,* 185.
3. Eaton, M. T. and M. H. Peterson (1969). "Psychiatry."
    Medical Outline Series. Medical Examination Publishing
    Co., Inc., 2nd ed., 267.
4. Marshall, Wallace (1970). "Immunologic psychology and
    psychiatry." *Journal of The Medical Association of The
    State of Alabama* 39:654.
5. Krech et al. *Elements of Psychology,* 310.
6. Pikunas, J., E. J. Albrecht and R. P. O'Neil (1969). *Human
    Development: A Science of Growth.* McGraw-Hill, N. Y.,
    413.
7. Aldrich, C. K. (1966). *An Introduction to Dynamic Psychi-
    atry.* McGraw-Hill, N. Y., 269.

Chapter 13

1. Marshall, Wallace (November 1972). "A psychiatrist raises
    the devil." *Journal of The Medical Association of The
    State of Alabama* 42:356-58.
2. *Colliers Encyclopedia* (1965). Crowell-Collier Publishing
    Co., vol. 8, 166.
3. *Encyclopaedia Britannica* (1959). Benton, Chicago, vol. 7,
    283-84.

4. Marshall, Wallace (September 1969). "Id, ego and superego revisited." *Journal of The Medical Association of The State of Alabama* 39:243-49.
5. ———. (September 1969). "Immunologic augmentations for learning and psychiatry." *Journal of The Medical Association of The State of Alabama* 39:243-49.
6. ———. (January 1969). "Immunologic psychology and psychiatry." *Journal of The Medical Association of The State of Alabama* 39:649-55.

Chapter 14

1. Marshall, Wallace (June 1971). "How people and places affect our behavior." *Medical Times* 99:203-10.
2. Pikunas et al. *A Science of Growth*, 40.
3. Marshall, Wallace (June 1973). "Immunologic interpretation of psychologic and psychiatric therapies." *Journal of The Medical Association of The State of Alabama* 42:898.

Chapter 15

1. Krech et al. *Elements of Psychology*, 292, 305, 611, 551-52, 596-601, 600-01.
2. Freedman, A. M. and H. I. Kaplan (1967). *Comprehensive Textbook of Psychiatry*. Williams and Wilkins Co., Baltimore, 509-38 (Zygmut Piotrowski) and 539-40 (Herbert Fensterheim).

Chapter 16

1. Marshall, Wallace (1973). "Immunologic interpretation of psychologic and psychiatric therapies." *Journal of The Medical Association of The State of Alabama* 42:850.
2. Hartley, David (1973). *Encyclopaedia Britannica*. Benton, Chicago, vol. 11, 135.
3. Priestley, Joseph (1775). *Hartley's Theory of the Human Mind, on the Principles of the Association of Ideas with Essays Relating to the Subject of It*. London, printed for J. Johnson, No. 72, St. Paul's Church Yard.

4. Marshall, Wallace (August 1950). "Mental research yester-year and today." *Medical Times.*

5. Vide (1), vol. 15, 459-63.

6. Koestler, A. (1964). *The Act of Creation.* Macmillan Co., N. Y., 3rd printing, 45.

7. Marshall, Wallace (September 1970). "Immunologic factors in psychosomatic disorders." *Journal of The Medical Association of The State of Alabama* 40:167-71.

8. Marshall, Wallace (January 1969). "Learning and development of frustrations." *Journal of The Medical Association of The State of Alabama* 38:622:25.

9. Pearson, M. M. (1963). *Strecker's Fundamentals of Psychiatry.* J. B. Lippincott Co., Philadelphia, 6th ed., 223.

10. Noyes, A. P. and L. C. Kolb (1963). *Modern Clinical Psychiatry.* W. B. Saunders Co., Philadelphia, 6th ed., 508.

11. Krech et al. *Elements of Psychology,* 784.

12. Sawry, J. and C. Telford (1971). *Psychology of Adjustment.* Allyn and Bacon, Boston, 3rd ed., 424-39.

13. Holden, C. (16 March 1973). "Psychosurgery: legitimate therapy or laundered lobotomy? *Science* 178:1,109-12.

14. Marshall, Wallace (June 1970). "The psychology of being hurt." *Journal of The Louisiana State Medical Society.*

15. Tan, L. T., Margaret Y-C Tan and J. Vieth (1973). *Acupuncture Therapy.* Temple University Press, Philadelphia, 8-9.

16. Marshall, Wallace (January 1970). "Immunologic psychology and psychiatry." *Journal of The Medical Association of The State of Alabama* 39:649-57.

Chapter 17

1. Marshall, Wallace (April 1969). "Theory, learning and the origin of complexes." *Journal of The Medical Association of The State of Alabama* 38:916-21.

2. Marshall, Wallace (January 1969). "Learning and the development of frustrations." *Journal of The Medical Association of The State of Alabama* 38:622-26.

3. Solomon, H. C. Personal communication, 25 November 1968.

4. *Dorland's Illustrated Medical Dictionary,* 1965, 24th ed.,

1,353.

5.   Ibid., 800.

6.   *Webster's New Collegiate Dictionary*. G. and C. Merriam, Springfield, Mass., 1953, 881.

7.   Braithwaite, R. B. (1964). *Scientific Explanation: A Study of the Function of Theory, Probability and Law in Science.* The University Press, Cambridge, 1.

8.   Ibid., 2.

9.   Vide No. 3, 277.

10. Wolman, B. (1965). In *Scientific Psychology: Principles and Approaches.* Basic Books, Inc., N. Y., 14.

11. Engel, G. L. (1965). *Psychological Development in Health and Disease.* W. B. Saunders Co., Philadelphia, 4, 5.

12. Bailey, P. (1965). In *Conditioning Therapies.* Edited by Wolpe, J., A. Salter and L. J. Reyna. Holt, Rinehart and Winston, Inc., N. Y., 64.

13. Thigpen, C. H. and H. M. Cleckley (1965). In *Conditioning Therapies.* Edited by Wolpe, Salter and Reyna. Holt, Rinehart and Winston, Inc., N. Y., 96.

14. Bailey, P. (1965). *Sigmund the Unserene.* Chas. C. Thomas, Springfield, 29.

15. *Webster's New Collegiate Dictionary,* 32.

16. Marshall, Wallace (1953). *Essentials of Medical Research.* Vantage Press, N.Y.C. (preface), vi.

17. ———. "Theory, learning and the origin of complexes."

18. ———. "The immunological concept of learning." 193-98.

19. Fuller, J. L. (29 December 1967). "Experimental deprivation and later behavior." *Science* 158:1,645-52.

Index